Celebrities
Serve

Celebrities Serve

"A Celebrity Tennis Cookbook"

to benefit

THE INTERNATIONAL TENNIS HALL OF FAME

By
DEE GORDON
DE LORA MAURUS
SHIRLEY GOROSPE

Cover photograph by Christopher Lawrence
Cover styling by Sara Barbaris
Cover food preparation by Plantation Catering, Newport, Rhode Island
Antique bench courtesy of Devonshire, Newport, Rhode Island

Left: The grass courts of the International Tennis Hall of Fame, Newport, Rhode Island
Photo by Ron Manville

ACKNOWLEDGEMENTS

We, the authors, would like to take this opportunity to thank all the tennis personalities, celebrities and professional players, as well as those behind the scenes at the Tennis Hall of Fame who have helped make this project a reality.

Our deepest gratitude goes to Mary Parker of the Hartford Publishing Group, without her guidance this book would have never reached its potential. Thanks also to Sara Barbaris of her staff for her design and the styling of the cover photograph. A special thanks to Richard Gordon for his expertise and support.

We would also like to thank the following professionals: Michael Baz, Carol Newsom, Christopher Lawrence and Ron Manville for their photography on behalf of this book; Martha Stewart and Susan Magrino from Crown Publishers, Inc. for their contributions and guidance; Jane Brown, George Gowen, Mark Stenning, Ellen Marshall, Christine Fontana and particularly Jan Armstrong, the librarian, and all the staff of the International Tennis Hall of Fame for their efforts; Bill Corcoran for his legal counsel; Carol Smith and Chris Hartley of Plantation Catering in Newport, Rhode Island. We must not forget to mention our special friends Gene Scott, Bill Talbert and Bud Collins from the board of the Hall of Fame for all their assistance and encouragement in this venture; Peggy Michael and her staff at the Grand Champions Cup in Indian Wells, California. Thanks to the staffs of the Screen Actors Guild, Advantage International, ProServ, IMG, and Nancy Bolger at Virginia Slims Tennis. Thanks also to Bill Faude for his wit and input.

The authors of this book hope you enjoy the recipes of your favorite tennis personalities. We also hope this book enhances and encourages your entertainment possibilities revolving around your love of the great game of tennis.

It is also our goal to acquaint the world of tennis with the unique and historic importance of the International Tennis Hall of Fame in Newport, Rhode Island. The attractiveness and character of the Newport Casino structure that permanently houses the Hall of Fame is a source of immense pride. Therefore, we dedicate this book to the International Tennis Hall of Fame. Any profits from the sale of this book will be donated to the Hall of Fame.

Dee Gordon
De Lora Maurus
Shirley Gorospe

Additional copies of CELEBRITIES SERVE can be obtained by writing to:

CELEBRITIES SERVE
Chefs To The Court
28 Mt. Vernon Street
Newport, R.I. 02840

or by filling out the order form found in the back of this book.

Please enclose your return address with a check made payable to Chefs To The Court in the amount of $15.95 per book plus $4.00 postage and handling per book. Rhode Island residents add $1.12 per book for sales tax.

Printed in the USA by

WIMMER BROTHERS
A Wimmer Company
Memphis • Dallas

TABLE OF CONTENTS

When it comes to competitive sports, tennis has always been my favorite. When I am out on the court, I feel a true sense of camaraderie with my opponent or opponents, if the game happens to be doubles. Following a week of hectic business, I look forward to sharing this invigorating activity of established rules, clad in the familiar uniform of crisp tennis whites.

Tennis always makes me think of lightness and brightness. I prefer playing outdoors during the cool morning hours when my body and mind are well rested. At this time the earth, too, is renewed and fresh and there is a wonderful awareness of nature's awakening.

Tennis for me, is a stimulating game of concentration and anticipation. I enjoy the "popping" sound that the ball makes when slammed with the racket, and I feel so satisfied when I return the ball and place it just where I intended it to land. Tennis is a great workout that combines aerobics, stretching, and toning, and with all of this, comes the knowledge that I am improving my game as I am perfecting my technique.

After a lengthy time on the court, it's so nice to share a good meal. Being conscious of body and health, my thoughts turn again to lightness and brightness. I want a menu that is refreshing, colorful, and nutritious. I like to serve a tennis repast on a table dressed with a white linen tablecloth and navy linen napkins. I set the table with white dishes and cobalt Depression glass, and accentuate it with seasonal flowers. No matter if I win or lose at tennis, I am pleased to present a simple yet elegant meal, continue with my company, and partake in good food and stimulating conversation.

Martha Stewart

HISTORY
of the International
Tennis Hall of Fame

"Newport Society"

Probably published in a *Harper's* magazine in the 1890's

I n the very heart of Newport stands a building -- the Newport Casino -- that is both a milestone in the history of American architecture and a symbol of the incessant mingling of new money and old, that has helped Newport to survive and flourish since its founding. When it was built, the very word casino was a novelty in America; it didn't imply professional gambling rooms, but rather a country club-like place in which people would gather on social occasions to eat, dance, play cards, listen to music and enjoy other innocent entertainment.

The idea of a casino for Newport had been talked about for several years. In the summer of 1879, James Gordon Bennett, Jr., smarting from snubs by "polite" society for his uncouth behavior (relieving himself in the fireplace in front of his fianceé), brought the idea to reality while seeking revenge. Bennett was the heir to *The New York Herald* and well-known for wild, impetuous and generally intoxicated behavior. He once challenged a visiting British army officer friend to ride a horse into the staid and prestigious Newport Reading Room. A few days later the *Newport Mercury* reported that Bennett had purchased land on Bellevue Avenue across from his own house with the intention of building a "new club house" for Newport summer fun. Bennett formed a joint stock company and offered shares in his product, at $500 each, to a select number of friends. The list of shareholders reads like a reprint of the Social Register. For the architectural work, he commissioned the firm of McKim, Mead and White; Stanford White, the junior member, was to be primarily responsible for the form the Casino would take.

What White brought from his drawing boards was a three-building complex in which space was provided for a bowling alley, a billiard parlor, reading rooms, restaurant, a court-tennis court, a theater-ballroom, bachelor lodgings and, on the ground floor facing Bellevue Avenue, space for shops to be occupied by "first-class tenants."

"Casino Building, Newport, R. I."
Bellevue Avenue Facade Elevation
Ink on linen/paper
McKim, Mead and White Archts.
57 Broadway, New York City
1879-80

The main building is three stories high, brick-faced at the street level, fish-scale shingles above. A paneled entryway on Bellevue Avenue led to the wonders within -- the neatly kept tennis courts, trees, shrubs, and pathways, the semicircular Horseshoe Piazza and a yellow-faced clock on a bulbous tower that

"Lawn Tennis Tournament Play"
Newport Casino
1880's

struck one viewer as a copy of a London bobby's helmet. Actually the tower is shaped after a form common to the Loire Valley of France, a region much favored by White. If on the Bellevue Avenue side the building bears a strong resemblance to a block of shops designed at about the same date by Richard Shaw in Bedford Park, London, on the courtyard side it shows that McKim and White were also aware of certain popular architectural influences that had arrived in the United States from the Far East. A display of Japanese buildings and furnishings at the Centennial Exposition in Philadelphia in 1876 had helped to create a fad for objects in the Japanese style -- fans, parasols, floor mats and the like -- that spread at once from coast to coast, manifesting itself in camps in the Adirondacks, as well as in the suburbs of Chicago.

"Lawn Tennis at Newport - The Tournament From the Upper Balcony of the Casino"
Photographed by Alman, Newport
Newport Casino
Published in *Harper's Weekly* September 5, 1885

The boldly turned wooden spindles and peek-a-boo openings of the lattices at the Casino (almost certainly designed by Stanford White) embraced this Japanese style, and the look was employed not only in the Casino but in several Newport houses that his firm designed during the period. The cost of the entire Casino was said to be close to $200,000.

"Spectators for Tennis Tournament Play"
Newport Casino
1890's

The grand opening was held on July 28, 1880, and the *Newport News* proclaimed "There is nothing like it in the old world or new." Within a week the Casino held a gigantic housewarming attended by more than 3,000 persons, an occasion the *Providence Journal* decreed as "the greatest event of its kind ever known here."

After socializing, tennis quickly became the Casino's leading sport. The game had been growing in popularity among the American elite since it first appeared

"United States National Lawn Tennis Tournament"
Men's Singles
Hovey vs. Smith
August 22, 1891

in this country from England, by way of Bermuda, around 1874. When, in 1881, the newly formed United States Lawn Tennis Association decided to hold its first national championship, the honor of serving as host for the event went to Newport and, of course, the Casino was the location of choice.

The sturdy old Casino continues to serve as the lively heart of Newport. In 1954, the first Newport Jazz Festival was held within its sacred precincts. At the same time, president of the Casino and originator of the VASSS No-Ad Scoring System, James Van Alen, secured sanction from the United States Tennis Association to create the International Tennis Hall of Fame at the Newport Casino.

The museum at the Casino has numerous tennis artifacts in the upper rooms. In one case, one may observe some of the most famous racquets ever used. Encased here is the racquet Chris Evert used to win the 1982 U.S. Open, right next to the tennis shoes she used to win the 1983 French Open Crown. Retired here is Jimmy Connor's Wilson T-2000, an antiquated species,the very one that helped him win the U.S. Open in 1983. So is "Big Bill" Tilden's wooden Bancroft bludgeon. It teamed with him to win the 1932 U.S. Open.

In the Enshrinee Room is everything you ever wanted to know about the 157 immortals who have earned a place in tennis history. In the central hallway, lined with art, are cases loaded with tennis trophies engraved with the accomplishments of players who had to settle for material goods rather than for the cash showered upon those for whom they paved the way.

The Casino also houses a court-tennis court. Court tennis, also known as real or royal tennis, is a unique game of great age and distinction. In its glory in six-

"Invitation Lawn Tennis Tournament"
Newport Casino
Finals: M. McLoughlin vs. R. Williams II (winner)
1915
This was the first Invitation Lawn Tennis Tournament contested at the Newport Casino. It took the place of the U.S. National Championships, which moved to the West Side Tennis Club in Forest Hills, New York, and attracted the same fine caliber of players.

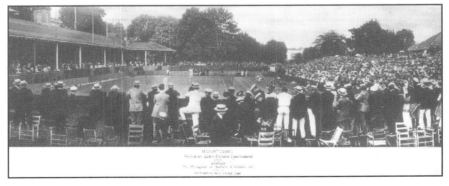

teenth-century Europe, it was the most important and obvious predecessor to lawn tennis, the game now known simply by its ancestor's name of tennis. This court tennis facility is one of only thirty-four in the world.

Today the Casino has thirteen grass tennis courts, which are the longest continuously used competition grass tennis courts in the world, the only such courts in the country open to the public for play. Croquet and court-tennis can also be played at the Casino for a fee.

The stately buildings with their latticed porches, immaculate courts, and beautifully landscaped grounds have all been restored to their original elegance. The tradition has been preserved, and today the Hall of Fame belongs to all tennis enthusiasts and will continue to thrive with the support of the world of tennis. The authors of this book cordially invite all fans of tennis to visit this extraordinary landmark.

"The Hall of Fame is something more than a lovely physical property. It is an inspiration for the young, setting them a goal that can be attained only through the sacrifice, perseverance and strength of character that won a place for those already enshrined there. Sport still has its ideals. None are loftier than those represented by The Tennis Hall of Fame." -- Allison Danzig, in his Citation for Enshrinees, 1955.

Left: The first International Tennis Hall of Fame enshrinee medal - a gold and sterling replica of the original medal, presented to America's first tennis champion, Richard Sears, in 1881, at the Newport Casino. The Hall of Fame presented this replica of the Sears medal for the first time to the 1987 enshrinees at July 18 ceremonies, held at the Newport Casino - home of the International Tennis Hall of Fame. All photos and illustrations courtesy of the International Tennis Hall of Fame, Newport, Rhode Island. Page 11: Palm Beach Tennis Club Championship Trophy. Photo by John Hopf

HALL OF
FAMERS

*T*here are 157 men
and women who have been
inducted into the
International Tennis Hall of
Fame. This chapter
includes recipes from some of
the "greats" of the game.

Preceding page:
U. S. National Singles Championship Trophy
Photo by John Hopf

Arthur Ashe

My favorite meal is a small Caesar salad, Saint Germain Soup, grilled swordfish, baby peas, white rice, lemon meringue pie, mint-flavored iced tea and Alka Seltzer - I've included the recipe for Saint Germain Soup - enjoy!

SAINT GERMAIN SOUP

1 pound split peas
1 quart water
1 medium onion, peeled and chopped
1 celery stalk, chopped
3 cups milk
Salt
Pepper
Croutons

Rinse and sort peas, then drain. In a 4 quart saucepan, bring to a boil peas, water, onion and celery. Simmer for about 2 hours. Stir occasionally to prevent sticking. Add milk, salt and pepper and cook until the soup is the consistency you desire. Garnish with croutons.

Don Budge

FEIJOADA
A BRAZILIAN DISH

¾ pound jerked beef
3 cups black beans
1 pound smoked sausage
1 pound smoked pork
1 pound smoked tongue
¹/₄ pound bacon
1 pig's foot
1 shallot, chopped
1 onion, chopped
1 piece fresh sausage, cut up
1 garlic clove, minced
Dash of cayenne pepper

Soak jerked beef overnight in plenty of cold water. Soak beans overnight. Drain beef, cover with cold water, bring to a boil for 15 minutes. Drain again and cool. Add all meats except the fresh sausage, cover with tepid water, bring to a boil and simmer until meats are almost tender. Meanwhile, in another pot, place the drained beans, cover with cold water and no seasoning and cook until almost tender.

Combine contents of the 2 pots and cook beans and meats together, simmering until meats are very tender and beans are soft enough to mash. While the meats and beans are cooking, fry shallots and onions with sausage until lightly browned, then add garlic and pepper. Stir, frying until lightly browned. Add 1 cup of cooked beans, mix well and mash all together, then stir in some of the bean liquid and simmer 5-10 minutes, until seasonings are blended. Return this sauce to the beans and meats and simmer until well blended. Adjust seasoning. Separate the meats from the beans and slice in uniform pieces and arrange on a platter. According to a long established custom, the tongue is placed in the center with the other meats surrounding it. Moisten the meats with some of the liquid from the beans. Serve the beans in a hot tureen, with fluffy boiled rice, sliced oranges, pepper and lemon sauce.

Right: Enshrinement Luncheon July 16, 1988
International Tennis Hall of Fame
Photo by Ron Manville

New Sweden 88   July 16, 1988
USTA Wing, Tennis Hall Of Fame
Cream of Cucumber Soup
Caesar Salad
Sliced Tenderloin
Roasted New Potatoes
Garden Vegetables
Buffet Dessert
on the Horseshoe Piazza
Banana/Strawberry/Heathbar Trifles
Assorted Cakes and Tortes
Platter of Fresh Fruits
International Coffee and Liqueurs
Champagne~ Cordon Negro Brut
by Friexenet

Catered by Michael's

Music
Dick Johnson's Swingshift Band

Evonne Goolagong Cawley *Enshrined 1988*

Any fish that has been frozen, soak in milk to get out the fishy frozen taste.

TERIYAKI FISH

Cobia fish, cut in thick chunks
Teriyaki sauce

Marinate in Teriyaki sauce for 2 hours, then barbecue on the grill. Serve with a nice tossed salad.

Joseph F. Cullman 3rd   *Enshrined 1990*

SAUTE OF CHICKEN BREASTS PRIMAVERA

4 tablespoons unsalted butter
6 large mushrooms, stemmed and thinly sliced
Salt and freshly ground white pepper to taste
3 whole chicken breasts, skinless, boned and cut in half
All-purpose flour for dredging
2 teaspoons peanut oil
½ to ¾ cup chicken stock or bouillon
1 cup heavy cream
Juice of 1 large lemon
1½ teaspoons beurre manie (made by rolling 1 tablespoon soft butter
**   with a tablespoon flour in a ball)**
½ cup fresh peas, cooked
2 to 3 tablespoons finely minced fresh dill or chives

In a small skillet, melt two tablespoons of the butter over medium high heat. Add the mushrooms and saute quickly until they are lightly browned. Season with salt and pepper and set aside.

Dry chicken breasts thoroughly on paper towels and season with salt and pepper. Dredge lightly in flour, shaking off the excess. Reserve.

Melt the remaining butter in a 12-inch iron skillet, together with the oil, over high heat. Add the chicken breasts and saute until nicely browned on both sides. Add about a quarter cup of stock, reduce the heat to medium-low and simmer, covered, for five minutes, adding a little more stock if it has evaporated significantly, until the chicken is done. The juices should run pale yellow. Remove the chicken breasts from the skillet and set aside.

Add a quarter cup of stock to the skillet, bring to a boil, whisking, and reduce by a quarter. Add bits of beurre manie, and whisk until the sauce lightly coats the spoon. Taste and correct the seasoning.

Return the chicken breasts to the skillet together with the mushrooms and peas and just heat through. Transfer the chicken to a serving dish, spoon the sauce over and garnish with the dill or chives. Serve at once with a crusty loaf of French bread. Yield: six servings.

Jaroslav Drobny

Enshrined 1983

Tvaroh/Czech cheese, which is called for in the recipe, is hard to get, so cottage cheese may be used instead.

CZECH FRUIT DUMPLINGS

8 ounces mixed flour and fine semolina flour
1 egg
4 ounces milk
Dash of salt
Fruit for filling: plums, apricots or strawberries, stemmed and pitted

Garnish:
2 ounces butter
2 ounces hard cottage cheese
1 ounce sugar

In a large bowl mix flour, semolina, egg, milk and salt until a soft elastic dough is formed.

Turn onto a floured board and lightly roll out and cut into squares. Place fruit on the squares, roll up in a ball and throw into boiling water for 5 to 8 minutes. Drain and serve sprinkled with sugar and grated hard cottage cheese and pour melted butter over each.

Margaret Osborne duPont
Enshrined 1967

TENNIS CLUB SPECIAL

1 onion, chopped
2 tablespoons light olive oil
1 pound ground round
1 package regular size corn chips
½ head of lettuce, sliced
1 tomato, cubed
1 cup mild cheddar cheese, grated
1 can taco sauce - mild, medium or hot

Saute onion in olive oil. Add meat, breaking apart with spoon while cooking and mix well with onion. Avoid over-cooking.

Lay bed of corn chips on plate. Spoon hot meat mixture onto chips. Top with lettuce, tomatoes and cheese. Add taco sauce as desired.

Roy Emerson
Enshrined 1982

PAVLOVA
AN AUSTRALIAN DESSERT

4 egg whites
8 tablespoons sugar
1 teaspoon cornstarch
1 teaspoon malt vinegar
Whipped cream
1 teaspoon vanilla
Powdered sugar

Preheat oven to 250 ° F. Grease and flour a sheet of foil on a cookie sheet.

Beat egg whites and slowly add the sugar. Beat until firm and able to form peaks. Add cornstarch and vinegar.

Turn out onto the cookie sheet and use a spatula to form meringue into a round bowl with high sides and a flattened center. B ake in oven for 1 hour. If browning too much, reduce heat. Leave in oven until cool.

To serve, add whipping cream, whipped with 1 teaspoon vanilla and a little powdered sugar. Decorate with passion fruit, strawberries or raspberries.

Neale A. Fraser

Enshrined 1984

A do-ahead creamy seafood curry.

SALMON CURRY CREME

1 large onion
2 ounces shortening
2 tablespoons plain flour
2 teaspoons curry powder
Salt and pepper to taste
Water to mix
1⅔ cups (14½ ounce can) evaporated milk
3 hard-boiled eggs, sliced
1 15-ounce can salmon
paprika

Preheat oven to 350° F. Grease a casserole dish.

Dice the onion finely, melt the shortening, add the onion and cook without browning until tender. Mix the flour, curry powder, salt and pepper to a thin paste with the water. Add evaporated milk. Stir into onion. Cook, stirring until thickened. Stir in the eggs and drained, flaked salmon. Place in greased casserole. Sprinkle with the cheese and a little paprika. Bake in a moderate oven for 15 to 20 minutes. Serve with buttered rice, sweet corn and peas. Serves 4.

Shirley Fry-Irvin

Enshrined 1970

CHICKEN SOUP-STEW

1 small piece chicken fat
6 chicken bouillon cubes
6 cups water
4 large chicken breasts
6 celery ribs
6 carrots
3 large potatoes, diced
1 large bay leaf

1 teaspoon sweet basil
1 can chicken soup, creamed
1 can celery soup, creamed

In a large Dutch oven melt the chicken fat and then add the cubes, water, and chicken breasts. Bring to a vigorous boil making sure the cubes are dissolved and then cook at a low heat until chicken is done (about an hour). Remove chicken from pot and dice. Place the chicken bones back in the pot and simmer while finely slicing the carrot and celery as well as preparing the potatoes. Remove chicken bones and add the celery and carrots, sweet basil and bay leaf. Allow all to cook until tender. Add the soups and let cook stirring constantly until all lumps disappear. Add potatoes and chicken and let cook until tender. You may have to add water. If so, thicken ½ cup cold water with 1 teaspoon cornstarch and shake well. Salt to taste, but good without. Can be frozen.

Variations:
If you like it hot and spicy, try 1 teaspoon mustard and/or curry powder. Rather than potatoes, thin the pot liquid and add dumplings.   Start with basic recipe and use any variety and combinations of vegetables -- lima beans, green beans, Chinese pea pods, 2 small cut up tomatoes.   Or use thyme with vegetables. Use your own imagination and wondrous things and odors emanate from the kitchen.

Slew Hester

CORNED BEEF AND CABBAGE

1 already corned brisket of beef, or equivalent, 1½ to 2½ pounds
2 tablespoons sugar
1 tablespoon pickling spices
1 tablespoon whole cloves
1 tablespoons onion, dried and chopped
1 tablespoon cinnamon
1 head of cabbage, cut in wedges

Place brisket in large covered pot with sufficient water to cover it. Add sugar, spices, cloves, onion and cinnamon. Boil for 1 hour covered. Reduce heat and simmer for 2 additional hours. Place cabbage in pot with meat and steam for 30 to 45 minutes or until cooked to taste.

Lew Hoad

TAGLIATELLE WITH BLUE CHEESE SAUCE

1 pound green tagliatelle
Salt and pepper
½ pint heavy cream
4 ounces Danish blue cheese (or French or Italian as long as it's blue)
2 ounces walnuts, chopped

Cook the tagliatelle in a large saucepan of boiling salted water for 10-12 minutes until just tender. Drain and place in a serving dish. Keep warm. In a saucepan, over very low heat, heat the cream. Crumble the Danish blue with your fingers and add to the cream. Add the chopped walnuts and season well.

Heat until the cheese has melted and the sauce is hot. Do not let the sauce boil or it will curdle. Pour the sauce over the tagliatelle and serve immediately.

FIGS IN SYRUP

Put 2 cups water in saucepan, add 1 cup cognac (cooking kind, not Remy Martin!), 2 tablespoons brown sugar or honey, a stick of cinnamon or ½ teaspoon of powdered cinnamon. Bring to boil, throw in 1 pound dried figs and simmer for 45 minutes to 1 hour. Let figs cool in syrup and serve with plain ice cream or cream. Don't eat the cinnamon stick.

Helen Hull Jacobs

"My cooking ability is practically nil, but this is the recipe for one of my favorite desserts."

CREME BRULEE

2 cups heavy cream
4 egg yolks, well beaten
Brown sugar or maple sugar

Boil cream for exactly 1 minute. Remove from fire and pour slowly into beaten egg yolks. Beat constantly. Return to fire. Stir and cook over flame until nearly boiling - or stir and cook for 5 minutes in double boiler. Place cream in greased baking dish. Chill well.

Cover cream with ⅓ inch layer of sugar. Place under broiler keeping oven door open, to form a crust and caramelize the sugar. Chill again.

Cream may be made one day and caramelized the next.

Billie Jean King

Enshrined 1987

CHEESY POTATOES

2 pounds frozen hash browns
¾ cup melted butter, divided
1 teaspoon salt
½ cup onions, chopped
1 can cream of chicken soup
1 pint sour cream
2 cups grated cheddar cheese
2 cups crushed corn flakes

Preheat oven to 350 ° F. Butter a 3 quart casserole or a 13" x 9" baking dish.

Slightly thaw potatoes. Combine with ½ cup melted butter and salt. Add chicken soup, onions, sour cream and cheese. Blend thoroughly. Pour into casserole. Mix cornflakes with ¼ cup butter and sprinkle over potatoes. Bake for 45 minutes. For main dish, add 3 cups ham, chicken or turkey. (May be made the night before.)

George Lott

MANICOTTI

Sauce:
1-1 pound and 13 ounce can tomatoes
1-6 ounce can tomato paste
1½ cups water
1½ cup white wine
1 bay leaf
½ teaspoon oregano
½ teaspoon salt
¼ teaspoon pepper
2 tablespoons brown sugar
1 pound ground beef, cooked and drained
1 clove garlic

Filling:
2 pounds ricotta cheese
½ pound mozzarella cheese, grated
½ cup parmesan cheese, grated
2 eggs
½ teaspoon salt
¼ teaspoon pepper
2 tablespoons chives, chopped
2 tablespoons parsley, chopped
One package manicotti (about 16 pasta "tubes")

Preheat oven to 350 ° F.

Combine sauce ingredients and simmer very slowly for 2-3 hours, adding more water if needed. Parboil manicotti for 3-4 minutes in salted water. Combine all cheeses with eggs and seasonings, chives and parsley. Mix well and stuff into pasta tubes with a table knife. Arrange in a flat baking dish, pour sauce over stuffed pasta and bake for 35 minutes.

Alastair B. Martin

Enshrined 1973

CHICKEN OR TURKEY PEANUT CURRY (THAILAND)

Chili paste:
1 red chili
½ onion, diced
1 clove garlic, diced

2 tablespoons butter
2 cups milk
1 pound chicken or turkey, cooked and sliced
1 cup peanut butter
2-3 teaspoons salt

Make chili paste by blending red chili, onion and garlic. Warm pot, add butter, mix in chili paste, milk, chicken, peanut butter and salt. Stir well. Serve with any mixture of rice -- brown, wild, etc. and beans and/or salad. This curry is good served with mango chutney.

Frankie Parker

Enshrined 1966

MUSHROOM STUFFED MEATLOAF

1 large onion, chopped
½ cup celery, chopped
2 tablespoons butter
1 pound medium mushrooms, sliced
¾ cup tomato juice
1 cup bread crumbs
1½ teaspoons salt
¼ teaspoon freshly ground pepper
½ cup sour cream
2 pounds ground chuck
½ tablespoon cumin
2 eggs beaten

Preheat oven to 450° F.

Saute onions and celery in butter. Add mushrooms and saute until vegetables are limp. Add ½ cup tomato juice. Simmer 10 minutes. Mix in bread crumbs, ½ teaspoon salt, ⅛ teaspoon pepper, and cumin. Add sour cream.
Mix ground meat with remaining salt and pepper, remaining tomato juice and eggs. Shape meat into loaf in greased pan. Scoop out center - fill with mushrooms and pat over mushroom stuffing. Bake for 20 minutes. Reduce oven to 350° F, and bake 30 minutes longer.

Fred Perry

THURGAU APPLE CAKE

3½ ounces butter, at room temperature
5½ ounces granulated sugar
4 eggs, separated
Pinch of salt
1 teaspoon lemon zest, grated
2 tablespoons lemon juice
5 ounces plain flour
1 teaspoon baking powder
3 medium-large apples, preferably Golden Delicious
Icing sugar (confectioners sugar)
Whipped cream (optional)

Preheat oven to 375 ° F. Grease a 10 inch springform pan.

In small bowl, beat butter and 1 ½ ounces of the sugar until light. Beat in eggs, one at a time, add salt, lemon zest, lemon juice (do not worry if mixture curdles).

Beat egg whites until soft peaks form, gradually adding 3 ½ ounces of the sugar, until firm. Blend ⅓ of the whites mixture with the butter-yolk mixture. Gradually incorporate the remainder with a rubber spatula.

Sift the flour and baking powder into the mixture, folding gently. Scoop into springform pan.

Peel, halve and core the apples, then cut into crosswise slices. Arrange them overlapping closely to cover the cake, pressing lightly into the batter. Sprinkle with the remaining granulated sugar.

Bake in center oven for about 45 minutes, or until a cocktail stick or skewer poked into the center comes out clean. Cool on a rack and unmold. Serve warm, lightly sprinkled with icing sugar. Offer whipped cream alongside if you like.

Variations: Other fruit such as peeled peaches, apricots, cherries or tender pears can be used.

Dennis Ralston

Enshrined 1987

A Christmas Eve tradition in the Ralston home.

Gram's Lady Finger Pudding

1 envelope unflavored gelatin
2½ cups milk
¼ teaspoon salt
1½ cup sugar, plus 1 tablespoon sugar
3 eggs, separated
1-8 ounce can crushed pineapple, drained
1 cup canned apricots, finely chopped
1 maraschino cherry, plus 2 tablespoons cherry juice
1 teaspoon vanilla
1 cup whipping cream
1 dozen or more ladyfingers, preferably fresh

Soak gelatin in 1 cup of milk.

Scald 1 ½ cups milk, salt and 1 cup sugar in double boiler. Beat yolks, adding ⅛ cup scalded milk. Pour into remaining scalded milk and heat until it coats a spoon - about 2 minutes - stirring constantly.

Remove from stove, pour into soaked gelatin and mix. Add pineapple, apricots and cherry juice. Cut mixture for marbled effect. Put above mixture into trifle bowl.

Beat egg whites with ½ cup sugar. Add 1 teaspoon vanilla. Layer on top of custard mixture in trifle bowl.

Whip cream with 1 tablespoon sugar. Layer on top of egg white mixture in trifle bowl.

Push ladyfingers down into the layers, around the edge of the trifle bowl. On top, use remaining ladyfingers to create a flower with the maraschino cherry for the center.

Frank Sedgman

COLD CHICKEN IN MUSTARD SAUCE

1 teaspoon dry, English-style mustard
Enough water to mix it to a paste
1 tablespoon prepared mustard
1 teaspoon white vinegar
1 large chicken (4 pounds, or 2 small ones)
1 tablespoon butter
1 tablespoon plain flour
1½ cups chicken stock
3 tablespoons cream

Mix the mustards together with the vinegar. Rub the skin of the chicken with the mustard mixture. Save remaining mustard mixture and refrigerate chicken for 24 hours.

Preheat the oven to 350 ° F.

Cover the chicken with a large piece of buttered foil. Place in casserole or baking dish. Pour 3 cups water into the dish, adding a little salt. Place in a moderate oven, covered with foil, until quite tender. Keep liquid and skim fat from the top.

Melt butter, add flour and cook 1 minute. Add stock and stir constantly until thickened. Cook a few minutes and then add cream and check for seasoning. Mix this gradually into the reserved mustard mixture and leave to cool. Cut the chicken into pieces and arrange on a platter. Spoon the mustard sauce over the top and leave to set. Decorate with chopped parsley and keep cold. This will set quite firmly.

Pancho Segura

SEAFOOD FETTUCCINE WITH GARLIC AND MUSHROOMS

½ cup olive oil
½ cup garlic, minced
½ cup fresh parsley, finely chopped
¼ cup fresh basil
1 pound fresh mushrooms, sliced
½ cup dry white wine
Dash of tabasco
1 cup Italian tomatoes, chopped (canned)
½ tablespoon chicken stock
½ tablespoon beef stock
1 cup cooked lobster, chopped
1 cup cooked shrimp
1 cup cooked crab, chopped
1 pound fettuccine noodles
¼ pound sweet butter

In a large skillet, add olive oil and saute the garlic, green onions, parsley and basil. Add the mushrooms, saute for a few minutes then add the wine, tabasco and tomatoes. Bring to a boil, add the chicken and beef stocks. Let simmer gently. Add seafood, simmer until just heated through. Boil fettuccine until al dente. Drain. Add butter, then sauce, and top with a little parsley. Serve immediately. Serves 8.

Vic Seixas

Enshrined 1971

CHEDDAR CHEESE WREATH

1 pound white cheddar cheese, grated
1 cup chopped walnuts
¾ cup mayonnaise
4 green onions, minced
1 clove garlic, minced
½ teaspoon tabasco

Mix all ingredients well. Spread in a ring mold. Refrigerate for 3 hours. Fill center with strawberry preserves and serve with crackers.

Stan Smith

Enshrined 1987

CREAMY BAKED CHICKEN BREASTS

4 whole chicken breasts, split, skinned and boned
8 (4 x 4) slices Swiss cheese
1 10¾-ounce can cream of chicken soup
¼ cup dry white wine
1 cup herb seasoned stuffing mix
¼ cup butter, melted

Preheat oven to 350 ° F. Lightly grease a 13" x 9" x 2" baking dish.

Arrange chicken in baking dish. Top with cheese slices. Combine soup and wine, stirring well. Spoon sauce evenly over chicken; sprinkle with stuffing mix. Drizzle butter over crumbs. Bake for 45 to 55 minutes.

Fred Stolle

GOODIES COOKIES

1 stick margarine
1 cup graham cracker crumbs
1 12-ounce package chocolate chips
1 12-ounce package butterscotch chips
1 can condensed milk
1 cup pecans, finely chopped

Preheat oven to 350 ° F.

Pour melted margarine into 9" x 13" Pyrex or metal pan. Sprinkle the graham cracker crumbs evenly over the margarine. Sprinkle the chocolate chips and then the butterscotch chips. Spread milk evenly over the mixture. Top with crushed pecans and take spatula and press mixture. Bake for 20 to 25 minutes. Be sure to cut into desired squares while it is still warm, but leave in the pan until completely cooled. Makes about 3 dozen.

Bill Talbert

VEGETABLE CLAM CHOWDER

1 package frozen peas
1 package frozen spinach, chopped
1 package frozen carrots, sliced
1 package frozen kernel corn
1 stick margarine or butter
3 cans minced clams
Pepper to taste
1 teaspoon sage
1 teaspoon thyme
½ pint heavy cream

Undercook all the frozen vegetables, drain and put in a big pot. Add the clams, butter and spices. Heat. At the last minute add the heavy cream and cook to a slight boil. Serve immediately with croissant (oven warm), wheat crackers and cheese. This chowder makes a delicious meal and is very satisfying though not filling. Serves 6.

Lance Tingay

Enshrined 1982

TROUT WITH TOMATO AND BASIL

2 fresh trout
2 tablespoons olive oil
1 clove garlic
4 small ripe tomatoes, cut in half, juice and seeds drained
4-5 leaves of basil
salt and black pepper

Clean the trout, rinse and drain well. Dry on kitchen paper. Heat olive oil in large pan and soften, without browning, chopped garlic. Put in trout, turning once in hot olive oil. Spread pulped tomato around trout. Sprinkle with salt and pepper. Tear up basil leaves and sprinkle on top. Cover pan with lid and simmer in low oven for about 12 minutes. Serve with boiled potatoes (preferably small new potatoes in their skins) over which olive oil has been poured. Serves 2.

Ted Tinling

Enshrined 1986

PINEAPPLE CASSEROLE

1 cup sugar
½ cup butter
4 extra large eggs
1 15½-ounce can crushed pineapple (undrained)
5 slices white bread, cut into small pieces

Preheat 350° F. Grease a 1 ½ quart casserole.

Cream sugar and butter together in large bowl. Add eggs one at a time beating well. After each one add some pineapple. Fold in bread. Pour into casserole dish. Bake uncovered for 1 hour. Serve warm or chilled with ham, pork or turkey.

Tony Trabert

BRONZINI

6 steamed chicken breasts, save broth
1 cup uncooked wild or long grain rice
Salt to taste
2 10-ounce packages frozen broccoli, thawed
2 cans cream of chicken soup
1 cup mayonnaise
1 teaspoon curry
2 tablespoons lemon juice
½ cup sharp cheddar cheese, grated
1 cup herb seasoned croutons

Preheat oven to 350 ° F.

Remove chicken from bones and cut in cubes. Cook rice according to package directions using chicken broth in place of water. Salt thawed, uncooked broccoli to taste. Combine soup, mayonnaise, curry, lemon juice and cheese. Put broccoli in bottom of 3 quart casserole. Heap on cooked rice, then cubed chicken and top with soup mixture. Bake 30 minutes. Cover with croutons and return to oven for 10 minutes. Serves 8.

Right: Harper's magazine
illustration of the
Tennis Hall of Fame

James Van Alen

Enshrined 1965

"Of course, it goes without saying, a bottle of champagne per couple to enliven the conversation and guarantee the utmost appreciation of this recipe."

A RECIPE GUARANTEED TO SATISFY THE APPETITES OF ALL

White chicken or lobster, diced and cooked
Wild rice
Powdered curry
Crisp bacon, crumbled
Miniature meatballs
Chutney and curry sauces, to taste

Using the rice as a base, sprinkle remaining ingredients on top and season to taste.

Ellsworth Vines

Enshrined 1962

LOIN OF PORK IN RED WINE

1 pork loin (3 to 4 pounds)
1 teaspoon salt
½ teaspoon pepper
¼ teaspoon sage
Nutmeg
2 tablespoons oil
¼ cup onions, chopped
¼ cup parsley, chopped
1 bay leaf
1 cup dry red wine
Whole onions
New potatoes, unpeeled
1 cup canned beef broth

Preheat oven to 350 ° F.

Rub pork with salt, pepper, sage and nutmeg. Brown in a little oil on top of the stove. Transfer to a rack in a roasting pan and add onions, parsley, bay leaf and wine. Roast in oven for 2 hours. Arrange whole onions and new potatoes in a lightly oiled baking pan and place in the oven. Roast meat and vegetables 40 minutes longer. Add broth to pan containing meat. Arrange the partially cooked vegetables around the meat and roast 20 minutes longer.

SPINACH SALAD

About 1 pound spinach leaves, washed
6 slices lean bacon
½ cup simple syrup*
½ cup vinegar
1 medium red onion, cut into thin slivers
1 teaspoon salt
2 teaspoons sugar
½ teaspoon coarsely ground black pepper
1 teaspoon Worcestershire sauce

Make simple syrup.

Rinse and dry spinach leaves. Tear and place in a large salad bowl. Cut bacon into pieces about 1 inch square. Fry until cooked but not crisp. Stir in simple syrup and vinegar; keep warm. Toss spinach with onion. Sprinkle with salt, sugar, pepper and Worcestershire sauce; toss again. Pour contents of skillet (bacon and seasoned drippings) over spinach and toss lightly, just enough to coat leaves.

* Simple syrup: combine 3 parts sugar and 1 part water. Boil 5 minutes, then cool.

Virginia Wade

Enshrined 1989

GRILLED SWORDFISH

1½ to 2 pounds swordfish steak
1 clove garlic, minced
1 tablespoon squeezed lemon juice
¼ cup olive oil

Mix together the garlic, oil and lemon juice in a shallow pan. Marinate swordfish for at least 1 ½ hours, turning occasionally.

Broil swordfish over charcoal for 5 to 8 minutes on each side. Do not overcook.

LAWN TENNIS CHAMPIONSHIP
OF THE
UNITED STATES
1914
· WOMEN'S SINGLES ·
FIRST PRIZE
WON BY
MARIE WAGNER

PROFESSIONAL
TENNIS PLAYERS

*T*his chapter includes recipes from the current players on the men's and women's professional tennis tour. Many of these players are future Hall of Famers. A player must have been out of serious competition for five years before being considered for induction into the International Tennis Hall Of Fame.

Andre Agassi

CHALUPAS

6 corn tortillas
1 cup cooking oil
½ pound ground beef
1 tablespoon bacon drippings
½ teaspoon cumin
¼ teaspoon chili powder
1 teaspoon salt
1½ cups bean dip
2 cups monterey jack or cheddar cheese, grated
Pepper to taste
6 teaspoons onions, finely chopped
¾ cup chopped, drained tomatoes
¾ cup iceberg lettuce, finely chopped
¾ cup guacamole
6 tablespoons sour cream

Preheat oven to 350 ° F.

Fry each tortilla in hot oil until crisp. Drain on paper towels and set aside. Saute meat in bacon drippings. Add cumin, chili powder and salt. Remove from heat. Spread each tortilla with ¼ cup bean dip. Layer about 2 tablespoons meat mixture on top. Sprinkle ⅓ cup of the grated cheese over the meat. Place on cookie sheet and bake until heated through, about 10 minutes. While piping hot, place on individual plates. Sprinkle each chalupa with pepper, 1 teaspoon onion, 2 tablespoons tomatoes, ½ cup lettuce, 2 tablespoons guacamole and 1 tablespoon sour cream. Serve immediately. If you are serving a crowd, put garnishes on table. Prepare each chalupa with bean dip, meat and cheese. Then let guests build their own.

Matt Anger

Banana Bread

¼ cup shortening
¾ cup sugar
2 eggs
2 cups biscuit mix
2 large or 3 small bananas, mashed
⅓ cup nuts, chopped (optional)

Preheat oven to 350 ° F. Grease a 9" x 5" loaf pan.

Cream shortening and sugar. Combine remaining ingredients and mix until well blended. Pour into prepared pan. Bake for 50 minutes. Cool on rack.

Lea Antanopolis

My Mom's Spanikopita

4 large bunches of fresh spinach
2 pounds feta cheese
1 pint cottage cheese
Salt and pepper to taste
6 eggs, beaten
Phyllo pastry
1 pound butter (might not use all of it)

Preheat oven to 350 °.

Clean spinach leaves to salad size and dry thoroughly by blotting with paper or regular towel. Combine feta cheese and cottage cheese together. Add salt and pepper. (Salt need not be added if feta is salty. I like a lot of pepper.) Add eggs to cheese mixture and mix together. Add cheese mixture to spinach (or vice versa) and use hands to coat spinach completely. In a lasagna pan (greased) put down one layer of phyllo pastry. Cut and shape pastry so it covers the sides of the pan also. Coat thoroughly with melted butter. Repeat this step until you have 4 layers of pastry. Pour spinach mixture into pan on top of pastry and spread evenly. Top mixture with 4 more layers of pastry each buttered and tucked into sides of pan. Cook for 45 minutes or until top is golden brown. If it's getting brown too early, cover with foil and finish cooking. Serves 8-10.

Jimmy Arias

Peach Cobbler

1 can peaches, quartered
1 stick butter
1 cup self-rising flour
1 cup sugar
1 cup milk
Vanilla ice cream (optional)

Preheat oven to 400 ° F.

Place 1 stick of butter in bottom of rectangular baking dish (baking dish should be about 3 inches deep). Put in oven until butter melts. In bowl, mix the flour, sugar, milk and beat well with a whisk. Pour mixture over melted butter (don't mix) and spoon peaches over batter mixture. Add only a small amount of juice from can. Very Important: Do not stir peaches into batter. Bake 35-40 minutes until top becomes golden brown (the mixture comes up around the peaches and turns golden brown). Serve hot.

V.J. Armitrage

DATE AND GINGER CHUTNEY

4 ounces dates, sliced and stoned
2 ounces fresh ginger, peeled and cut into matchstick-size strips
4 ounces fresh, ripe mango, peeled and thinly sliced *or* 2 ounces dry
    mango pieces
2 ounces raisins and currants mixed
1 ounce almonds, chopped
⅔ cup water
6 ounces sugar or jaggery, a solid palm sweetener
¼ teaspoon salt
1 teaspoon red chili powder

Put dates, ginger, fresh or dry mango, currants and almonds into a saucepan.
Add water. Keep aside for 6-8 minutes. Add sugar or grated jaggery, salt and
chili powder and simmer gently. Cook for 15 to 20 minutes until chutney is
thick and sticky. Remove, cool and serve. It can be bottled and kept with or
without refrigeration for up to 3 months.

SWEET TOMATO CHUTNEY

1 ounce ghee (clarified butter) or 1 tablespoon oil
1 inch cinnamon stick
1 bay leaf
6 cloves
1 teaspoon mustard seed
1 teaspoon chili powder
¼ teaspoon turmeric powder
2 ounces sugar
1 pound fresh or canned tomatoes
2 ounces raisins
½ teaspoon salt

Heat ghee or oil and fry cinnamon, bay leaf and cloves for 1 minute. Add
mustard seed. When they begin to crackle, add chili, turmeric and sugar. Mix
well and add tomato. Mix well and add raisins and salt. Cover and simmer for
8-10 minutes. Add a little water if liquid thickens. Tomato chutney should have
medium consistency. Serve hot or cold. Once cooked it can be bottled or kept
in refrigerator for up to six weeks.

Tracy Austin

Chocolate Mousse

8 ounces chocolate, melted in double boiler
6 tablespoons sweet butter, softened
Pinch of salt
3 eggs
½ cup superfine sugar
1 cup cream, whipped

Beat together chocolate, butter and salt. Separate eggs and add yolks to chocolate mixture. Then beat. Beat 3 egg whites until a stiff consistency is reached. Gradually add ½ cup superfine sugar until it stands in peaks. Fold chocolate mixture into egg white mixture, then fold in whipped cream. Refrigerate.

Jennifer Capriati

Gourmet Peanut Butter and Jelly Sandwich

2 pieces of bread
2 tablespoons extra crunchy peanut butter
2 tablespoons grape jelly

Spread peanut butter evenly over one piece of bread, spread jelly evenly over the other piece of bread then slap together. With a sharp knife, trim off all the crust. Cut sandwich diagonally in quarters and garnish with carrots.

Pat Cash

Pat Cash ate at least 10-12 muffins a day during the 1987 Wimbledon Championships. He won Wimbledon that year.

Bran Muffins - The Muffin of a Champion

1 cup flour (wholemeal or plain)
1 cup raisins
1 cup nuts
½ teaspoon nutmeg
1 teaspoon cinnamon
1 cup bran
1 cup skim milk
1 teaspoon baking powder
1 egg

Preheat oven to 350 °. Prepare muffin cups.

Soak bran in milk. Combine all ingredients and pour in bran mixture. Bake for 20-25 minutes.Recipe may be varied by adding different fruit of your choice, or use oats or oat bran as well. This is just a basic recipe.

Jimmy Connors

My favorite meal: Chicken Fried Steak, Mashed potatoes, Green Beans and Lemon Meringue Pie. My mother always made me eat everything on my plate before I'd get any Lemon Meringue Pie.

CHICKEN FRIED STEAK

1½ - 2 pounds round steak, ½ inch thick
2 eggs, beaten
2 tablespoons milk
1 cup fine cracker crumbs
¼ cup fat
Salt and pepper

Cut steak into serving pieces. Pound steak thoroughly, or ask butcher to do it. Mix eggs and milk. Dip meat into egg mixture, then cracker crumbs. Brown slowly on both sides in hot fat. Season with salt and pepper. Cover tightly, cook over very low heat 45-50 minutes or until tender. Makes 6 servings.

Jimmy Connors (continued)

Lemon Meringue Pie

1½ cups sugar
3 tablespoons cornstarch
3 tablespoons all purpose flour
Dash of salt
1½ cups of hot water
3 slightly beaten egg yolks
6 tablespoons sugar
½ teaspoon grated lemon peel
2 tablespoons butter or margarine
⅓ cup lemon juice
1 9-inch baked pastry shell
3 egg whites
1 teaspoon lemon juice

In a saucepan mix sugar, cornstarch, flour and salt. Gradually blend in water. Bring to a boil over high heat, stirring constantly. Reduce heat to medium, cook and stir 8 minutes more. Remove from heat. Stir small amount of hot mixture into egg yolks, return to hot mixture. Bring to a boil over high heat, stirring constantly. Reduce heat to low, cook and stir 4 minutes longer. Remove from heat. Add lemon peel and butter. Gradually stir in ⅓ cup of lemon juice. Cover entire surface with clear plastic wrap. Cool 10 minutes. Now pour into cooled pastry shell. Cool to room temperature (about 1 hour).

Preheat oven to 350° F.

For meringue, beat egg whites with lemon juice until soft peaks form. Gradually add sugar, beating, until stiff peaks form and sugar is dissolved. Spread meringue over filling, sealing to edges of pastry. Bake for 12 to 15 minutes or until meringue is golden. Cool thoroughly before serving.

Stefan Edberg

SWEDISH MEAT BALLS

¾ **pound lean ground beef**
½ **pound ground veal**
¼ **pound ground pork**
1½ **cups soft bread crumbs**
1 **cup light cream**
½ **cup onion, chopped**
3 **tablespoons butter**
1 **egg**
¼ **cup parsley, finely chopped**
1½ **teaspoons salt**
¼ **teaspoon ginger**
Dash each of pepper and nutmeg
2 **tablespoons all purpose flour**
¾ **cup canned condensed beef broth**
¼ **cup cold water***
½ **teaspoon instant coffee**

Have meats ground together twice. Soak bread in cream about 5 minutes. Cook onion in 1 tablespoon butter until just tender. Mix meats, crumb mixture, onion, egg, parsley and seasonings. Beat vigorously until fluffy (about 5 minutes at medium speed on mixer, then 8 minutes by hand). Form in 1 ½ inch balls (mixture will be soft - for easier shaping, wet hands or chill first.) Brown lightly in 2 tablespoons butter, shaking skillet to keep balls round (don't try to do too many at once). Remove meat balls.

Make gravy by stirring flour into drippings in skillet. Add broth, water, and coffee. Heat and stir until gravy thickens.

Return meat balls to gravy, cover, cook slowly about 30 minutes, basting occasionally. Makes 3 dozen 1 ½ inch balls.

*For creamy gravy, substitute 1 cup light cream and ½ teaspoon concentrated meat extract.

Chris Evert

VEAL AND MUSHROOMS

6 ounces of veal
1 medium onion
¾ stick of butter or margarine
2 cups consomme soup
1 cup fresh mushrooms
1 can of water chestnuts, drained

Preheat oven to 350 ° F.

Brown veal with onions in butter, add salt and pepper to taste. Place in casserole dish. Add consomme, mushrooms and water chestnuts. Cover and bake for 45 minutes.

Excellent with a noodle side dish.

Left: Chris Evert competing in the Virginia Slims Tournament, Newport, R.I. Photo by Michael Baz

Ros Fairbank

For 1 ⅛ pounds of meat, (beef, chicken or lamb) use the following ingredients:

MILD EASTERN CURRY

1 large onion
2½ tablespoons oil
4-5 teaspoons curry powder
1 peeled and sliced tomato
Pinch of salt
2 tablespoons dessicated coconut
1 cup water
2 tablespoons dried fruit
2-3 teaspoons peanuts, chopped
1 apple, cored, peeled and diced

Brown onion in oil, add curry powder and cook over low heat for a few minutes. Add meat and brown. Finally add the remaining ingredients and simmer for 1 to 1 ½ hours or until meat is tender.

This dish is best prepared the night before and left in the refrigerator until ready to serve. Reheat and serve over rice with sliced bananas and chutney.

Patricia Fendick

GARLIC SCALLOPS

1 pound scallops
2 tablespoons butter
3 scallions, diced
1 clove garlic, diced
½ cup mushrooms

Saute all ingredients and serve over white rice.

Anna-Maria Fernandez

ANTIPASTO SALAD

1 14-ounce can artichoke hearts
1 14-ounce can hearts of palm
1 cup celery, chopped
3-4 tomatoes, chopped
1 can water chestnuts, chopped
2 red peppers, chopped
2 zucchinis, chopped
1 small can olives, chopped
4-5 carrots, grated
10 12-ounces provolone cheese, grated
10 12-ounces mozzarella cheese, grated
Caesar dressing

Combine all ingredients, add Caesar dressing. Chill in refrigerator 30 minutes to 1 hour.

Gigi Fernandez

Puerto Rican Chicken Fricassee

1 pound chicken, cut into strips
2 tablespoons oil
2 strips bacon, finely sliced
1 onion, chopped
1 green pepper, chopped
3 cloves garlic, minced
3 tablespoons oregano
1 8-ounce can tomato sauce
1 16-ounce can stewed tomatoes
1 cube chicken bouillon
8 green olives
8 capers, drained
4 leaves cilantro
2 potatoes, peeled and quartered

Brown chicken in oil. Stir-fry bacon and add onion, green pepper, garlic, oregano and saute for about 10 minutes over medium high heat. Add tomato sauce and stewed tomatoes with 1 ½ cans water. Add bouillon, olives, capers, cilantro, potatoes and browned chicken. Simmer over low heat for 30 minutes or until potatoes are done.

Serve over rice.

John Fitzgerald

MY FAVORITE BROWNIES

4 squares unsweetened chocolate
1½ sticks butter
2 cups sugar
3 eggs
1 teaspoon vanilla
1 cup flour
1 cup chocolate chips

Preheat oven to 350 ° F. Grease a 9" x 13" pan.

Microwave chocolate and butter in large bowl on high 2 ½ minutes or until butter is melted. Stir until chocolate is well blended. Stir in eggs and vanilla until completely mixed. Mix in flour until well blended. Stir in chocolate chips. Spread in pan and bake for 35 minutes. Do not overbake. Cool in pan and cut into squares.

Sammy Giammalva

ITALIAN CREAM CAKE

½ cup margarine
½ cup vegetable shortening
2 cups sugar
5 eggs, separated
1 teaspoon baking soda
1 cup buttermilk
2 cups sifted flour
1 3⅓-ounce can angel flake coconut
1 cup pecans, chopped
1 teaspoon vanilla

Preheat oven to 350 ° F. Grease and flour three 9" layer pans.

Cream margarine and shortening then add sugar gradually. Add egg yolks and beat well. Add soda to buttermilk then add flour and milk alternately to cake batter. Add pecans and coconut. Fold in well beaten egg whites and vanilla.

Divide batter evenly into the three pans and bake each for 25 minutes. Ice each "layer" with cream cheese frosting and stack the layers. Top the cake with a sprinkling of chopped pecans if desired.

CREAM CHEESE FROSTING:

8 ounces cream cheese
¼ cup margarine
1 pound confectioners sugar
1 teaspoon vanilla
2 teaspoons milk
Chopped pecans, optional

Soften cream cheese and margarine, then cream together. Add sugar, vanilla and milk. This frosting is excellent with Italian cream cake.

Dan Goldie

CHRISTINE'S PASTA SALAD

12 ounces tri-colored pasta
1 medium onion, diced
3 chicken bouillon cubes, dissolved in 12 ounces boiling water
1 garlic clove, diced
1 pound boneless breast of chicken, cut into cubes
1 8-ounce can of water chestnuts, chopped
1 10-ounce bag frozen corn, cooked
2 cups broccoli florets, steamed
2 medium tomatoes, chopped
1 red bell pepper, chopped
1 yellow bell pepper, chopped
1 large cucumber, chopped
Onion salt, garlic powder, Italian seasoning and black pepper to taste
1 cup Italian dressing

Saute the onions in the chicken broth until soft. Add the mushrooms and continue cooking. When tender, add the diced garlic and the cubes of chicken. Watch the chicken carefully and cook just until white and tender. Do not overcook.

In a large bowl, combine the steamed broccoli, cooked corn, cucumber, tomatoes, bell peppers and water chestnuts. Stir until combined.

Add the chicken, mushrooms and onions (including the chicken broth) to the mixture of vegetables. Add the salad dressing and stir. Add onion salt, garlic powder, black pepper and Italian dressing, seasoning to taste. Toss well.

Serve either warm or cold.

Steffi Graf

Wiener Schnitzel

6 veal cutlets (5-6 ounces each), pounded thin
1 tablespoon fresh lemon juice
Salt to taste
Freshly ground black pepper
½ cup all-purpose flour
2 eggs
2 tablespoons cold water
1 cup fine dry bread crumbs
3-5 tablespoons butter
3 tablespoons vegetable oil
6 thin slices lemon
6 rolled anchovies
1 tablespoon drained capers

Sprinkle cutlets with lemon juice and let stand 30 minutes. Pat dry with paper towels and sprinkle one side of each cutlet lightly with salt and pepper. Dip cutlets into flour to coat both sides evenly, shaking to remove excess flour. In shallow bowl or pie plate, beat eggs and 2 tablespoons cold water together with fork until frothy. Place bread crumbs in similar bowl. Dip cutlets into egg mixture to coat both sides evenly, then dip into crumbs to coat both sides evenly. Place on waxed paper or plate.

Saute breaded cutlets, 2 or 3 at a time, in 3 tablespoons butter and the oil in a large skillet over medium heat. Cook until golden, 4-6 minutes on each side. Transfer to heated serving platter and keep warm in preheated 225 ° F oven while cooking remaining cutlets. Add remaining butter to skillet as necessary. Before serving, garnish each cutlet with lemon slice, anchovy and a few capers.

Serve with Spätzle as a side dish.

Peanut Louie Harper

CHOCOLATE CHIP COOKIES

¾ cup unsalted butter
⅔ cup sugar
⅔ cup brown sugar
1 egg
2 teaspoons vanilla
1½ cups flour
1 teaspoon baking soda
¾ teaspoon baking powder
¼ teaspoon salt
1⅔ cup rolled oats, ground to fine powder and set aside
1 12-ounce package chocolate chips

Preheat oven to 350 ° F.

Cream butter with both sugars. Add the egg and vanilla. Sift together flour, baking soda, baking powder and salt, then stir into creamed mixture. Stir in oats and chips. Bake until golden, about 8 minutes.

Aaron Krickstein

SOLE WITH GARLIC AND HERB BUTTER

2 pounds fresh filet of sole
1 stick melted butter
2 cloves garlic, minced
2 tablespoons chives, chopped
2 tablespoons parsely, chopped
2 tablespoons lemon juice

Preheat broiler.

Place sole filets in one layer in baking dish. Combine the remaining ingredients and drizzle over the fish. Broil for about 4-5 minutes or until fish flakes easily with a fork. Do not overcook. When serving, pour sauce on top. Serves 6.

John Lloyd

VERMONT BREAD

5-6 medium potatoes, peeled and cut
4 eggs
1 cup Vermont maple syrup
2 packages regular dry yeast
1 package oatmeal
4 sticks butter
Salt to taste if desired
5 pounds unbleached flour

Boil potatoes until tender. Do not add salt or butter. Put in blender and puree. Save the potato water. Cool potatoes, then add back the reserved water.

Add to the potatoes and water the eggs, syrup, yeast, oats, butter, salt and flour. Knead together adding flour as needed. When "dough consistency," put into large greased pan, cover with towel, put in warm place and allow to double in size. After dough has doubled, (about 1-1 ½ hours), turn out, knead again, adding flour as required, return to pan, cover again and allow to rise again. After doubling in size again, turn out, knead again, then cut into loaf-size portions. Keep in mind that these will need to double in size again, and take this into account when cutting the loaves, also keep them roughly half the size of the loaf pans. This dough can also be made into rolls, etc. If you want to get really "cutesy" take some of the dough, roll out to about ½-inch thick, butter and sprinkle with brown sugar and cinnamon, roll up and slice into 1-inch thick rolls. In bottom of a glass casserole-type dish, pack ½-inch of brown sugar and sprinkle with walnuts; sprinkle with enough water to make sugar damp (but not sloppy wet) and lay in the rolls; this variation makes "sticky buns."

Once you have the loaves, rolls or whatever you've formed, once again allow to rise to double, then put in pre-heated oven at 325 ° F and bake until golden brown -- usually takes about a half hour for rolls, 40 minutes or so for regular-size loaves, even more for large loaves. Test for doneness by thumping with finger -- should sound hollow. Turn out to cool. If you've made sticky buns, you'll need to turn upside down and remove dish within a few minutes or carmelized sugar will stick to dish rather than rolls. Forget everything about waiting until bread cools and rip off a piece, butter like you've never heard the word "diet" and enjoy a hot piece of bread. Almost as satisfying as winning Wimbledon!

Bob Lutz

SHARON'S CHICKEN ENCHILADAS

1 can golden mushroom soup
1 can cream of celery soup
2 8-ounce cans salsa
8 boneless chicken breasts
1 package cheddar cheese
1 package Monterey Jack cheese
1 can sliced olives
1 package corn tortillas

Preheat oven to 350 ° F.

Mix soup and salsa in a bowl. Cook chicken breasts. Grate cheese and mix. Put one layer tortillas in 9" x 13" casserole. Cover with shredded chicken and then cover with soup mix. Top with cheese and olives. Keep layering until casserole is full.

Bake for 45 minutes to 1 hour or bubbling. Let sit for 10 minutes. Cut into squares. Serve with sour cream and guacamole as topping. Serves 8.

Serve with rice and beans and garden salad. Also hot flour tortillas, Sangria or Margaritas.

Ivan Lendl

White Bread Dumplings

4 cups flour
1 teaspoon salt
2 egg yolks
1 ½ cup club soda water
4 cups stale white bread, diced

Sift flour into a bowl. In a second bowl, lightly beat together salt, egg yolks and soda water, pour in flour. Work dough until it is shiny and does not stick to the bowl. Cover and let stand for one hour. Work in the stale white bread with floured hands. Shape dough into three or four small sized rolls.

Bring about six quarts of water to a boil in a large pot. Cover and cook for about 10 to 15 minutes on each side. Remove from pan with a large skimmer. Make a cut across center of one of the rolls to make sure it is done. It will appear dry and porous when it is fully cooked. Slice into ¾ inch pieces with a thin sharp knife or a piece of thread. Serves 6 to 8.

Dill Cream Sauce

2 cups light cream
¼ cup flour
½ cup milk
1 egg yolk
1 tablespoon dill, chopped
Salt and vinegar to taste

Bring cream to boil. Pour in milk mixed with flour and egg yolk. Stir until it begins to thicken. Add dill and vinegar and salt to taste. Stir until well mixed.

Can be served on top of veal, chicken or beef.

Left: Ivan Lendl and his dog Todd
Photo by Michael Baz

Gretchen Magers

SNICKERDOODLES

1 cup shortening
1½ cup sugar
2 eggs
2 ¾ cup flour
2 teaspoons cream of tartar
1 teaspoon soda
½ teaspoon salt
2 tablespoons sugar
2 teaspoons cinnamon

Preheat oven to 400 ° F.

Cream together shortening, sugar and eggs. Add dry ingredients and mix well. Chill dough. Roll into balls the size of a small walnut. Then roll balls in a mixture of 2 tablespoons sugar and 2 teaspoons cinnamon.

Bake until brown and soft for 8-10 minutes.

Alberto Mancini

TORTELLINI ALFREDO

1 pound cheese tortellini, cooked
6 tablespoons sweet butter
1 cup cooked ham, cut in julienne
1 cup sliced mushrooms
½ cup heavy cream
½ cup grated parmesan cheese
¼ cup grated swiss or Gruyere cheese
Freshly ground pepper

Melt 2 tablespoons butter in skillet. Add ham and mushrooms. Saute over medium heat for 5 minutes. Then melt 4 tablespoons butter in medium saucepan. Add cream and heat until bubbly. Gradually add cheeses, beating constantly. When smooth, add ham and mushrooms. Toss with warm tortellini and serve immediately. Sprinkle with freshly ground pepper. Serves 2-3.

Hana Mandlikova

I like to call this Fettuccine a la Hana because I like to taste it to the last minute before I serve it. It is therefore difficult to explain exactly how much I put into the dish. It is a dish I like to eat often because the ingredients are healthy and are very rewarding for next day matches.

Fettuccine a la Hana

1 cup heavy cream
3 tablespoons butter
Fettuccine (fresh: 3 eggs and 2¼ cups flour)
Salt to taste
⅔ cup fresh parmesan cheese
Pinch of nutmeg

Combine ⅔ of the cream and the butter in a pan in which you can cook and serve. Heat for one minute until thickened.

Boil the fettuccine to a firm pasta. Drain and transfer to the pan with the sauce. On a lower heat toss fettuccine with the sauce, adding the remaining cream, parmesan cheese, salt, pepper and nutmeg.

Serve with cheese on the side.

Tim Mayotte

Black Forest Cake

½ **pound fresh dark sweet cherries, pitted** *or* **1 cup canned dark sweet**
    cherries, drained and pitted
8 tablespoons Kirschwasser
½ **cup sifted cake flour**
½ **cup sifted cocoa**
6 eggs, separated
1 ½ cups granulated sugar
1 teaspoon vanilla extract
½ **teaspoon salt**
½ **teaspoon cream of tartar**
5 tablespoons butter, clarified
Cocoa and butter
2 cups heavy cream, whipped
½ **cup powdered sugar**
Semisweet chocolate curls

Preheat oven to 350 ° F.

Combine cherries and 2 tablespoons of the Kirschwasser in small saucepan and let stand while preparing cake.

Sift together flour and cocoa. Beat egg yolks in small bowl with electric mixer on high speed until very thick and lemon-colored, about 5 minutes. Add ½ cup of the granulated sugar, vanilla and salt. Beat until sugar is dissolved and mixture forms a ribbon when beater is lifted, 2-3 minutes.

Wash and dry beaters thoroughly. Beat egg whites and cream of tartar in large mixer bowl at high speed until foamy, then gradually beat in ½ cup granulated sugar. Beat until stiff peaks form and sugar is dissolved.

Right:Tim Mayotte at the
Volvo Men's Tennis Tournament
Newport, R. I.
Photo by Michael Baz

Tim Mayotte *(continued)*

Gently fold dry mixture into yolk mixture. Fold 2 large spoonfuls of egg whites into yolk mixture. Pour yolk mixture over remaining whites and gently fold together just until blended. Gently fold in butter, about 2 tablespoons at a time. Divide batter evenly between 2 buttered and cocoa-dusted 8-inch round cake pans. Bake in oven until center of cake springs back when lightly touched, 25-30 minutes. Cool cake 5 minutes, carefully remove from pans and cool on wire racks.

Add 2 tablespoons water to cherries in saucepan. Heat to simmering over medium-low heat. Reduce heat to low and simmer until cherries are tender, about 5 minutes. Drain, reserving liquid. Heat 2 tablespoons of the liquid and remaining ½ cup granulated sugar to simmering in small saucepan over medium-low heat. Simmer until very syrupy, about 3 minutes. Remove from heat and stir in 4 tablespoons Kirschwasser.

Cut cake layers in half horizontally to make 4 thin layers. Drizzle syrup mixture evenly over cut sides of each layer, spreading with spatula to cover evenly.

Whip cream until soft peaks form, then add powdered sugar and 2 tablespoons Kirschwasser, beating until stiff.

Place 1 cake layer, cut side up, on plate. Spread with scant ¾ cup whipped cream. Top with second layer, cut side down, spread with scant ¾ cup whipped cream. Reserve 6 cherries for garnish and arrange remaining cherries over whipped cream on cake layers. Repeat process with third and final layers. Frost top and sides of cake with remaining whipped cream. Garnish with reserved cherries and chocolate curls.

Refrigerate until serving time.

John McEnroe

VEAL WITH PESTO AND PASTA

2 pounds boneless veal, cut from the leg or shoulder
Salt and pepper to taste
½ cup flour
2 tablespoons butter
2 tablespoons olive oil
4 shallots, finely minced
1 clove garlic, mashed
¼ pound prosciutto, chopped or shredded
½ cup chicken stock, homemade or canned
1 pound fresh peas
2 cups tightly packed fresh basil leaves
3 tablespoons pine nuts
1 tablespoon walnuts
2 cloves garlic, mashed
A dash of salt
½ cup oil
¼ cup parmesan cheese
½ cup ricotta cheese
1 cup heavy cream
1 pound thin spaghetti
2 tablespoons melted butter
Freshly grated Parmesan cheese

Cut the meat into small cubes and season with salt and pepper. Dredge the meat lightly in the flour and shake off the excess. (This works best if you sprinkle the flour over the meat in a colander and let the excess flour fall through.) Heat the butter and oil in a skillet and saute the cubes of meat until they are golden brown on all sides. Add the shallots, garlic and prosciutto and saute for another minute or two.

Pour in the stock, cover the skillet and simmer for 10 minutes or until the meat is tender.

Shell the peas and cook them in 1 inch of boiling, salted water for about 3 minutes. Rinse them under cold water to refresh them, and drain. (If you prefer, use one package of defrosted, frozen peas. It is not necessary to cook them.)

While the meat is cooking, put the basil leaves, pine nuts, walnuts, garlic and salt into the container of an electric blender or a food processor fitted with the steel blade and puree until smooth. Add the oil and blend well. Add the cheeses and mix for another few seconds. Do not overmix.

When the meat is tender, add the basil sauce, stir and add the heavy cream and the peas. Stir to combine. Cover the skillet again and allow the entire mixture to cook a few minutes longer to heat through.

Bring a large pot of salted water to a rolling boil and add a tablespoon of oil. Drop the pasta into the boiling water and cook it for 6 to 8 minutes if fresh, 10 to 12 minutes if dried. Drain the pasta and toss it with the melted butter.

To serve, toss the sauce through the pasta and pass additional grated Parmesan cheese.

Meredith McGrath

Wild Ginger Sesame Chicken Wings

1 cup sesame seeds, browned
3 cups soy sauce
1 teaspoon ground ginger
1 cup brown sugar
1 cup white wine
3 garlic cloves, crushed
4 dozen chicken wings, skinned

Preheat oven to 400 ° F. Brown sesame seeds on a cookie sheet in oven for 10 minutes - watch carefully to keep from burning.

OK now, cut the wings into 3 parts and throw away the tips. Combine soy sauce, ginger, brown sugar, white wine and garlic cloves in saucepan. Boil for 15 minutes. Dump in the wing parts and simmer for 15 minutes longer. Top with seeds, cover and refrigerate.

Preheat the oven to 400 ° F. Thirty minutes before serving bake the wings for 15 minutes.

When I make these, I <u>skin</u> the wing parts because the marinade really gets to the meat. This way you're not eating all the fatty, skin bits.

Lori McNeil

PORK VINDALOO

1 large onion, peeled and chopped
2 ounces ghee or 3 tablespoons oil
1 inch cinnamon stick
6 cloves
6 green cardamons
1 teaspoon ginger paste
1 pound garlic paste
1 pound lean pork, cut into cubes
3 tablespoons malt vinegar
1 teaspoon chili powder
1 teaspoon ground cumin
2 teaspoons ground coriander
3 tablespoons tamarind pulp
2 teaspoons tomato puree
2 teaspoons sugar
Water
2 sprigs fresh green coriander leaves, chopped
1-2 green chilis, chopped
Salt to taste
1 tablespoon oil for tempering
6-8 curry leaves

Fry onions in ghee or oil until light brown. Add cinnamon stick, cloves and cardamons. Fry for half a minute. Add ginger, garlic pastes and pork and fry for 5 minutes or until liquid from pork is dry. Add vinegar and chili, cumin, coriander, tamarind pulp, tomato puree and sugar. Cover and cook for 10-15 minutes. Add a little water if mixture is dry. Sprinkle with coriander leaves and chopped chili. Cook on low heat for 30-40 minutes or until pork is tender. The dish should have a rich gravy. Heat tempering oil and add the curry leaves. When leaves turn crisp and dark, pour the flavoured oil over the curry and cover. Mix well before serving. Serve with boiled rice.

Martina Navratilova

CHICKEN PAPRIKA

Salt and pepper
2 whole chickens portioned
3 tablespoons oil
2 cloves garlic
2 onions
2 tablespoons paprika
2 cups chicken bouillon
1 cup sour cream
2 tablespoons flour

Salt and pepper chicken. In a large pot, heat the oil, add garlic and onions. When they become pink, add the paprika. Add chickens and fry on each side stirring so the chicken doesn't burn. After 10 minutes add bouillon, cover and simmer for one hour. Remove chicken from pot. Mix sour cream and flour, add this sauce to the pot. Cover for a minute and then add the chicken that was removed earlier. Great with dumplings.

Yannick Noah

CHILI BEANS

1 tablespoon salad oil
2 medium onions, chopped
2 garlic cloves, minced
3 pounds beef chuck, coarsely ground
3 tablespoons chili powder
½ teaspoon dried oregano
1 teaspoon salt
1 can tomato paste (6-ounce)
1 can solid packed tomatoes (1 pound, 12-ounce), drained
2 jars sliced mushrooms (4½-ounce jars), drained

Heat oil in 8-quart pot. Lightly saute onions and garlic. Add meat, breaking up and stirring with wooden spoon until color changes. Add remaining ingredients. Stir, cover and simmer for 2 hours. Season to your taste.

Jana Novotna

FRUIT SMOOTHIE

½ can (6-ounce) frozen orange juice concentrate
1 small ripe banana, sliced *or*
1 cup fresh strawberries, sliced *or*
1 cup fresh peaches, sliced
½ cup skim milk
½ cup water
1 tablespoon honey
3 ice cubes

Combine the orange juice concentrate, fruit, skim milk and water in the container of an electric blender. Cover, whirl at high speed until thick and smooth for about 1 minute.

Add ice cubes, one at a time, and blend until smooth and frothy.

Right: Jana Novotna creating a
Fruit Smoothie
Indian Wells, CA
Photo by Michael Baz

Pascale Paradis

Not to be served with Coca-Cola ... best served with a Bordeaux wine.

Filet Of Duck In Greenpepper Sauce

1 duck filet
1 tablespoon butter
2 jiggers of Cognac
1 cup sour cream
1 squeeze of lemon
Salt and pepper
1 tablespoon green peppercorns

Gently fry the filet in butter until golden brown (6 minutes skin side - 4 minutes meat side). Add 1 jigger of Cognac. Put a match to it until the flame dies. Take out the filet and put it in a preheated oven, leave them to cook for 2-5 minutes (or until the meat is pink). Take sour cream, squeeze of lemon, pepper, salt and green peppercorns and warm very gently with the remainder of the Cognac and duck juice. (This must be on very low heat; if not, the cream will separate.)

Cut the filet in fine slices and pour the cream sauce over the top.

Serve with sauted potatoes or pasta, and Bordeaux wine.

Barbara Potter

FUDGE CAKE

2 cups dark brown sugar
1 stick (¼ pound) butter, melted
2 eggs
2 squares unsweetened chocolate, melted
1 teaspoon baking soda
½ cup boiling water
½ cup sour cream
1 teaspoon vanilla
1 cup flour, sifted

Preheat oven to 350 ° F. Grease and flour a 9" square pan.

Combine brown sugar, butter and eggs, and mix well. In small bowl combine chocolate, baking soda and boiling water. (When you pour boiling water on top of baking soda this will foam high in the small dish.) Add to sugar, butter and eggs. Then add sour cream and vanilla. Mix until sour cream is absorbed. Sift in flour and mix gently until absorbed.

Pour in pan and bake for 30 minutes. Center will be slightly wobbly when done – it will hold finger print rather than bounce back. Ice with favorite chocolate icing or sprinkle with powdered sugar.

Jim Pugh

MUSHROOM AND ADUKI CROQUETTES

¾ cup aduki beans, soaked overnight
2 tablespoons olive oil
¾ pound mushrooms, chopped
1-2 dried red chile peppers, seeded and diced
1 teaspoon ground cumin
2 tablespoons whole wheat flour
Salt and pepper to taste

Coating:
1 small egg, beaten
⅔ cup fine oatmeal
Oil for shallow frying

Drain beans, cover with fresh water and bring to boil. Boil for 10 minutes, reduce heat and simmer, covered, for 35-40 minutes or until tender. Drain and set aside.

Heat oil in a large pan and gently fry mushrooms, garlic, chili peppers and cumin for 5 minutes.

Sprinkle with flour. Continue cooking over low heat for 2 minutes, blending the flour in well. Remove from heat and mix in the beans, seasoning well. The consistency should be soft but not mushy. Chill for several hours or overnight.

Shape into 8 croquettes about ½ inch thick. Dip first into beaten egg and then into oatmeal. Fry in hot oil for 4-5 minutes on each side. Serve hot.

*Left: Jim Pugh helping out at the Volvo
Men's Tournament in Newport, R.I.
Photo by Michael Baz*

Richie Reneberg

MIMI'S BAR-B-Q'S AND SAUCE

1 pound ground beef

Sauce:
½ **cup chopped onion**
½ **cup chopped celery**
¼ **cup chopped green pepper**
¼ **cup chili sauce**
¼ **cup catsup**
1 cup water
½ **teaspoon pepper**
1 teaspoon salt
1 tablespoon Worcestershire sauce
2 tablespoons vinegar
2 teaspoons brown sugar
1 teaspoon dry mustard
½ **teaspoon paprika**
½ **teaspoon chili powder**
1 tablespoon chopped parsley

Brown ground beef and add the sauce. Simmer all ingredients for sauce gently until vegetables are cooked. Spoon onto buns and top with creamy cole slaw. Serve open face or top with other half of bun.

Stephanie Rehe

Simply Irresistible Cheesecake

Crust:
18-20 graham cracker squares, crushed
¼ cup brown sugar
¼ cup melted butter
½ teaspoon cinnamon

Mix and press into 10" springform pan.

Filling:
3 eggs
24 ounces cream cheese
1 cup sugar
½ teaspoon vanilla or 1 tablespoon light rum

Beat all ingredients together for 20-30 minutes (yes, 20-30 minutes). Pour into 10 inch springform pan lined with crumb crust.

Preheat oven to 350 ° F. Bake for 20-30 minutes.

Topping:
1 cup sour cream
3-4 tablespoons sugar

Mix together sour cream and sugar. Spread over top of baked cheesecake. Return to oven for 5 minutes. Let cool then chill.

Jo Anne Russell

There are a dozen varieties of avocado cultivated in South Florida. Some have lucious buttery fruit weighing up to 4 pounds. Avocados do not ripen until they are picked or fall from the tree.

SOUTH FLORIDA GUACAMOLE

Peel ripe but slightly firm fruit, about 1 ½ pounds, chop with knife or mash coarsely with a fork (be sure to have texture).

Spread over all:
3 tablespoons pimento or tomato, peeled and seeded, or both
2 tablespoons onion, grated
2 tablespoons key lime or lemon juice
Salt and dust with cayenne pepper to taste
4 tablespoons mayonnaise or sour cream

Mix lightly, taste and adjust. Cover tightly if for later use. Mix again, bring on the chips and dip, spread or serve with mild lettuce for salad.

Gabriela Sabatini

MALENESSA WITH PASTA - SABATINI

8 veal scallops, cut very thin and pounded to flatten out
1 cup milk
Olive oil
5 tablespoons butter
Salt and pepper
Paprika

Soak the veal in milk for an hour. Then brush them with olive oil and brown them well on both sides in butter. Lower heat and simmer gently until they are tender. Season to taste with salt, freshly ground pepper and paprika. Remove to hot plates and serve with lemon wedges and spaghetti dressed with butter and grated cheese. Serves 4, can be prepared in less than a ½ hour.

Larry Scott

Corn Bake

1 17-ounce can whole corn, do not drain
1 17-ounce can cream style corn
1 box corn bread mix
1 stick butter, room temperature
1 8-ounce container sour cream
1 egg

Preheat oven to 375 ° F. Grease a 9" x 9" baking dish.

Mix all of the ingredients together and put in baking dish. Bake for 40 minutes.

This is very fast and easy and delicious!

Monica Seles

CUSTARD FRUIT TART

1 cup all-purpose flour
¼ teaspoon salt
¼ cup cold margarine or butter
1 tablespoon shortening
1 egg yolk
3 tablespoons cold water
1 8-ounce package cream cheese, softened
½ of an 8 ounce carton vanilla yogurt (scant ½ cup)
¼ cup sugar
2 tablespoons orange juice
½ of a small papaya, peeled, seeded and thinly sliced
½ kiwi fruit, peeled and thinly sliced
½ cup blueberries
½ cup raspberries
½ cup seedless green grapes
¼ cup sliced strawberries
½ cup orange marmalade
1 tablespoon hot water

For crust, in a mixing bowl combine flour and salt. Cut in cold margarine or butter and shortening until mixture resembles coarse crumbs. Make a well in the center. Beat together egg yolk and cold water. Add egg mixture to flour mixture. Using fork, stir until dough forms a ball. Wrap in clear plastic wrap and chill 20 minutes in the freezer or 1 ½ hours in the refrigerator or until easy to handle.

Preheat oven to 375° F.

On a lightly floured surface, roll dough into a 12" or 13" circle. Fit into a 10-11" flan pan with removable bottom. Turn overhanging dough edges to inside and press against sides of pan. Bake for 25 minutes or until golden. Cool.

For filling, in a small mixer bowl, beat cream cheese, yogurt, sugar and orange juices until smooth. Spread mixture evenly over the cooled crust. Cover and chill at least 1 hour or until set. Just before serving, arrange fruit on top of filling. For glaze, combine marmalade and hot water. If desired, strain through a sieve. Spoon over fruit. Chill until serving time.

Pam Shriver

FAVORITE MORNING CEREAL CONCOCTION

½ cup each of 2 non-sugar varieties of cereal
½ banana, peeled and cut in small pieces
¼ cup seasonal berries
A few raisins
A sprinkle of cinnamon
½ small container of non-fat yogurt
Skim milk in desired amount

Mix all ingredients in a large bowl.

One newspaper and your day is underway. Herb tea and/or fresh fruit juice will help wash it down.

Left: Pam Shriver at Newport during the
Virginia Slims Tournament
Photo by Michael Baz

Liz Smilie

CHOCOLATE PUFF

1 tablespoon butter
½ cup sugar
1 tablespoon plain flour
1 tablespoon cocoa
2 egg yolks
2 egg whites
½ cup milk
Pinch of salt

Preheat oven to 300 ° F.

Cream butter and sugar. Add flour and cocoa which have been sifted together. Combine egg yolks and milk and add to creamed mixture. Add salt to egg whites and beat until stiff and fold in.

Spoon mixture into baking dish. Set dish in a large pan and pour hot water into the outer pan until it reaches the level of the batter. Cook for 1 hour.

Serve with whipped cream.

Helena Sukova

FRUIT DUMPLINGS

1 egg
9 ounces farmer's cheese
6 ounces flour
½ tablespoon butter
½ teaspoon salt
½ cup blueberries or strawberries, etc.

Mix egg, cheese, flour, butter and salt, to make a dough.

Wrap fruit in a thin layer of dough and drop into boiling water and boil for 8-10 minutes or until cooked (the dumplings will be floating on the surface of the water). Drain and serve immediately.

Sprinkle with sugar and cinnamon and melted butter; or sugar and farmer's cheese and melted butter; or sugar and ground poppy seeds and melted butter.

Jonas Svensson

Escalope de Saumon

2 pounds salmon filets
2 tablespoons melted butter
Juice of 1 lemon
2 shallots, finely chopped
½ cup white wine
⅔ cup heavy cream
1½ teaspoons dijon-style mustard
1½ teaspoons salt, or desired amount to taste
½ teaspoon freshly ground pepper

Preheat oven to 400 ° F.

Arrange salmon in a single layer in a large baking dish. Drizzle the butter and lemon juice over the fish. Place dish in the oven and cook, uncovered for about 10 minutes.

In a small saucepan, simmer shallots and wine over low heat until wine has evaporated and shallots are tender, about 8 minutes. Stir in cream, mustard, salt and pepper.

Pour over fish, return to oven and cook for additional 5 minutes, or until fish is glazed, but not browned. Serves 6.

Wendy Turnbull

Hope you can use this recipe - it's a favorite Australian dish.

COCONUT MACAROONS

1 cup coconut
½ cup sugar
1 tablespoon cornstarch
1 egg
Pinch of salt

Preheat oven to 350 ° F. Grease and lightly cornstarch cookie sheets.

Combine coconut, sugar and cornstarch in bowl. Beat together egg and salt, stir into dry ingredients. Mix well. Place heaping teaspoonfuls of mixture on cookie sheets. Press mixture lightly into macaroon shape, bake in moderate oven for 15 minutes or until golden brown. Remove cookies from cookie sheets immediately. Allow to cool on trays. Makes approximately 18.

Arantxa Sanchez Vicario

This dish is open to lots of variation, so do not be discouraged if one or two of the seafood ingredients are not available -- as you become more familiar with the recipe you can add other things you may wish to add such as cubed pork or halibut.

PAELLA

6 chicken legs
3 one pound live lobsters
1½ pounds fresh shrimp
24 mussels in shell
24 hardshell clams in shell
1 pound chorizo, sliced
1 quart chicken broth
½ teaspoon saffron

Right: Arantxa Sanchez Vicario
at the Virginia Slims Tournament
Newport, R.I.
Photo by Michael Baz

½ cup olive oil
2 cloves garlic, crushed
1 large onion, chopped
2 cups long-grain rice
2 teaspoons salt
Freshly ground black pepper
4 tomatoes, peeled and quartered or 1 one pound can, drained
1½ cups peas, fresh or frozen
1 4-ounce can pimentos, sliced

First prepare the shellfish. Remember to have the lobster cut up at the market. Peel the raw shrimp, leaving the tails on. Large-size shrimp, which run about 15 to the pound are easier to handle and you won't need to peel as many of them. Clean the clams and mussels thoroughly.

About an hour before dinner time, preheat the oven to 325 ° F. Put chicken broth on to boil. If you have homemade stock, so much the better, but you can use canned broth or broth made from bouillon cubes. When the broth comes to a boil, turn off the heat and add saffron.

Meanwhile, saute chicken legs in olive oil over medium heat until they are golden brown. Then put them aside in a covered dish to keep them warm and juicy. Add garlic and onions to oil and cook over low heat, stirring frequently, until the onion is translucent. Add rice and cook until it is translucent and faintly golden (absorbing the oil makes it so), stirring lightly with a fork. Add chicken broth, salt and pepper, and stir to loosen any browned bits at bottom of pan. Cover and simmer 10 minutes so that the rice will absorb some of the broth.

Into the largest casserole you own, or two small ones - rubbed with olive oil beforehand - put half of the uncooked shellfish, chorizo slices, tomatoes, peas and pimento. Arrange the chicken legs and the rest of the shellfish, chorizo, tomatoes, peas and pimento on top and spoon remaining rice and broth around these. Cover the casserole and bake for 30 minutes. Look in on it once or twice and if it seems too dry, add extra liquid. You may use extra broth if you have any or water if you don't, but it must be boiling, otherwise the temperature of the mixture will be lowered considerably, cooking time thrown off and the rice will be gummy. Remove cover and bake until rice is fluffy (about 10 minutes).

Mats Wilander

Grilled Shrimp in Lemon Butter Sauce

1 pound large raw shrimp
¼ pound butter
¼ cup olive oil
1 tablespoon parsley, chopped
½ teaspoon garlic, minced
¼ teaspoon oregano
¾ teaspoon salt
½ of 1 lemon

Preheat oven to 450 ° F.

Peel, devein and slice shrimp halfway through from head portion to tail. Place in a baking dish.

Melt butter and combine with oil, herbs and juice of lemon (can be made ahead to this point). Pour over shrimp and broil for 5 minutes at 450 ° F. Serve with brown rice.

Brown Rice

1 cup brown rice
3 cups chicken broth

Cook rice in chicken broth over low heat until rice is tender and absorbs all the liquid, about 45 minutes. Serves 4-6.

Tim Wilkison

Vegetarian Entree (Chicken may be added if desired)

1 cup uncooked rice (prepare according to directions)
3 medium zucchini squash
2 4-ounce cans green chilies
12 ounce monterey jack cheese, shredded
1 large tomato
2 cups sour cream
1 teaspoon garlic salt
1 teaspoon oregano
¼ cup green pepper, chopped
¼ cup onion, chopped
2 tablespoons parsley

Preheat oven to 350° F. Butter a 3-quart baking dish.

Cook zucchini until tender, drain and set aside.

In baking dish, layer rice, cover with chilies and sprinkle with ½ cheese. Add zucchini, tomato and ½ parsley. Combine remaining ingredients and add to dish. Bake for 45 minutes. Remove and sprinkle with remaining parsley. Serves 8.

CELEBRITY CHEFS

*T*he following
recipes were submitted by
personalities from film,
television and the political
arena. All share a love for the
game of tennis. Many play in
pro-am tournaments to
support their favorite charities.

Tony Bodner

Executive Chef, Disneyland Theme Park Operations

CREVETTES PROVENCALE

16 large shrimp, peeled and cut in half
¼ cup butter
¼ teaspoon seasoned salt
1 tablespoon shallots, finely minced
1 tablespoon garlic, finely minced
¼ teaspoon dried thyme leaves
½ cup Sauterne wine
2 whole ripe tomatoes, peeled and diced
Hot fresh cooked rice or noodles

Rinse and dry shrimp. Heat butter in large skillet or saute in pan until hot. Add shrimp and salt and stir for 1 ½ minutes. Add shallots, garlic and thyme, and cook 1 more minute. Add tomato and wine. Cook, stirring 1-2 minutes longer or until mixture is slightly thickened. Do not overcook. Serve with rice or noodles.

Nick Bollettieri

Tennis Coach

LAYERED MOZZARELLA AND TOMATO SALAD

4 large, ripe tomatoes, cut into ¼" slices
2 pounds fresh mozzarella cheese, cut into ¼" slices
¼ cup fresh basil, chopped
½ cup vinaigrette
Freshly gound black pepper to taste

On a large serving platter alternate overlapping slices of tomatoes and mozzarella. Sprinkle basil over all. Drizzle vinaigrette over salad and add pepper to taste.

Serve at room temperature. Serves 6.

Nicholas Brady

Secretary of the Treasury

COLD OR HOT BORSCHT

1 jar pickled beets with onions
2 cans beef broth
2 or 3 tablespoons sour cream

Drain liquid from jar and discard. Put drained beets and beef broth in blender (may also add some sour cream) and liquify. Chill or heat. Float 2-3 tablespoons of sour cream on top of the soup and serve.

Lloyd Bridges

Actor

CHEESE BUNS

6 whole hamburger buns
¾ cup cheddar cheese (half mozzarella can be used)
1 can condensed, undiluted tomato soup
1 small bottle pimento-stuffed olives
Grated onion to taste
1 teaspoon basil or oregano
(You can also add 2 or 3 tablespoons chopped jalapeno peppers)

Preheat oven to 350 ° F.

Cut small slice in top of buns and with a sharp knife and/or spoon, scoop out insides of buns (save tops). Cut cheese in cubes and place in sauce pan. Add remaining ingredients and heat slowly until cheese is melted, stirring as needed. Pour mixture into hollowed buns, place tops on buns and put buns onto cookie sheet. When ready to serve, reheat buns until tops are slightly browned and you can see that the cheese is bubbling.

This dish can be prepared in advance, except for reheating, and is convenient to make for luncheon or light supper entertaining. Can also be individually wrapped in foil and frozen.

Peter Burwash

Tennis Specialist

SPINACH LASAGNE

2 bunches spinach, chopped or 1 package frozen chopped spinach
½ pound cooked lasagne noodles (whole wheat or spinach noodles are tasty as well)
¼ pound mushrooms, sliced
1 tablespoon oil
4 cups favorite marinara or tomato sauce (2 15-ounce cans or jars of sauce)
¾ cup ricotta cheese or cottage cheese
¾ pound mozzarella cheese

Preheat oven to 375 ° F.

Steam fresh spinach until tender, or defrost frozen spinach until it can be broken apart. Cook lasagne noodles until tender and drain. Brown mushrooms in oil and add the sauce. (If adding spices, let this simmer.) In a large baking pan or casserole dish arrange in layers: lasagne noodles, spinach, cottage cheese or ricotta cheese and mozzarella. Cover with the sauce, seeing also that the sauce covers the sides of the casserole. Bake for 45 minutes.

Barbara Bush

First Lady

Vegetable Salad (spinach)

2 pounds fresh spinach, chopped
10 hardboiled eggs
1 pound bacon, cooked and crumbled
1 medium head of lettuce, shredded
1 cup shallots, sliced
1 package thawed frozen peas, uncooked

Place in order in layers in a large salad bowl.

2½ cups mayonnaise
2½ cups sour cream
Salt and pepper
Worcestershire sauce to taste
Lemon juice to taste

Blend together and pour over peas. Add ½ cup grated swiss cheese on top.
Cover and chill 12 hours. Do not toss. Serve.

Apple Crisp with Orange Juice

4 cups sliced pared tart apples
¼ cup orange juice
1 cup sugar
¾ cup flour, sifted
½ teaspoon cinnamon, ground
¼ teaspoon nutmeg, ground
Dash of salt
⅓ cup butter

Preheat oven to 375 ° F. Butter a 9" pie plate.

Mound apples in pie plate and pour orange juice over them. In separate bowl,
combine sugar, flour, spices and salt; cut into batter until mixture is crumbly.
Sprinkle over apples. Bake for 45 minutes or until apples are tender and topping
is crisp. Serve warm with cream.

Lynda Carter

Actress

Caesar Salad

4 large garlic cloves, peeled and pressed
2 filets of anchovy per person, split
A grating of black pepper
Juice of 1 lemon
2-3 tablespoons Worcestershire sauce
3-3½ teaspoons dijon-style mustard
1 part olive oil to ⅓ part vinegar
2 heads of romaine lettuce
1 egg
2-3 tablespoons parmesan cheese
Croutons

Salt bottom of wooden salad bowl. Add garlic, anchovy and black pepper. Work to paste. Add lemon juice, Worcestershire sauce and mustard. Work into bowl adding coarse black pepper to taste. Mix with vigor. Shake oil and vinegar on sides of bowl. Break lettuce into 2 inch lengths and place in salad bowl. Cook egg gently in simmering water 1 to 1 ½ minutes. Drop the egg from the shell into the ingredients in the bowl. Add croutons and cheese. Toss salad well and serve at once.

Bud Collins

Editor in Chief, World Tennis Magazine

Whenever I arrive in London the first thing I do is report for gustatory duty at a restaurant, a trattoria if you will, called Amato. I know I will be well fed in the Northern Italian manner, kindly received and find the price moderate. I have been doing this since 1970, eating there virtually every night during Wimbledon. This may indicate either that I don't have much of an exploring nature, or that I'm lucky to have found a place I can count on to conclude a long "working" day (better use quotes here in regard to my labors). Over the years the restaurant has changed names —Santa Croce, then Ziani Dolce, now Amato, for the boss, Luciano Amato, —while retaining high standards. Though not a great restaurant, this small place on the Chelsea Embankment at the end of Cheyne Walk, is a comforting refuge. Anyway, the dish I invariably order to lead off a London stay is Penne Arrabbiata. Arrabbiata means angry, indicating the spicy mood of the sauce in which the tubular pasta, penne, appears. But its hot taste immediately cools any ire I might be feeling.When he was the chef, Luciano often prepared this dish, which he details for us, Penne Arrabbiata for four persons.

PENNE ARRABBIATA

2 garlic cloves
4 tablespoons olive oil (preferably extra virgin olive oil)
1 tablespoon salt
¾ pound fresh tomato paste
½ chili pepper, chopped
4 or 5 basil leaves
Penne (or spaghetti)

Use a large frying pan for the sauce, which takes about 20 minutes altogether. Squeeze garlic into the pan with olive oil and salt. Heat over high flame until the garlic turns light brown. Then add tomato sauce, chili pepper and basil leaves. Lower the flame by about half and stir together. Meanwhile boil the penne (or spaghetti, or pasta of choice) in a nearby pot. Cook it al dente, then join it with the sauce in the frying pan, and heat together over a low flame for about a minute so that the sauce will adhere to the pasta. You may serve with basil leaves and parsely as garnish.

I hope you like it. If not, please don't be arrabbiata at me.

Kenneth Cooper

Father of aerobic exercise

GRILLED DIJON CHICKEN

4 skinless chicken breasts
2 teaspoons dijon mustard
¼ teaspoon black pepper
2 tablespoons diet margarine
2 teaspoons lemon juice
½ teaspoon garlic, minced
1 teaspoon dried tarragon

Wash chicken pieces and pat dry. Spread mustard on both sides of chicken and sprinkle with pepper. Cover and refrigerate for 4 hours. Melt diet margarine and stir in lemon juice, garlic and tarragon. Place chicken on grill, baste with sauce. Grill 40 to 45 minutes or until done. Turning and basting frequently. Yields 4 servings.

Serve with 1 medium potato baked, or 3 new potatoes, with topped "lite" sour cream and 1 teaspoon chives and 1 tablespoon grated cheese. Also serve 2 cups of green salad with dressing, and ½ cup fresh strawberries.

Bill Cosby

Actor

MONKEY BREAD

5-5½ cups all purpose flour
2 packages active dry yeast
⅓ cup sugar
1 teaspoon salt
½ cup water
½ cup milk
½ cup butter
3 large eggs
1 cup or more melted butter for dipping

Preheat oven to 375 ° F.

In large mixer bowl combine 1 ½ cups flour, yeast, sugar and salt. In saucepan heat water, milk and butter until warm at 120 to 130 ° F, butter need not melt. Add to flour mixture. Add eggs. Beat at low speed until moistened. Beat at medium speed for 3 minutes.

Add enough remaining flour to make soft dough. Knead on a floured surface for 8 to 10 minutes. Place in a greased bowl turning to grease top. Let rise in a warm place until light and doubled, about 1 hour.

Punch down and turn on floured board. Roll out ¼" thick. Cut dough into diamonds (with cookie cutter) or any shape preferred. Dip each piece into melted butter and arrange in a buttered "monkey pan" (10" tube). Cover and let rise again until almost doubled, about 1 hour. Bake for 45 minutes or until browned and done. Makes 1 loaf.

Cathy Lee Crosby

Actress

APPLE COBBLER CATHY LEE

5 pounds small red delicious apples
1 cup yellow raisins
1 teaspoon cloves
1 teaspoon nutmeg
Double pastry for a pan 12" x 18" x 2"
2 cups honey
1 cup fresh grated coconut
1 teaspoon cinnamon
3 teaspoon cornstarch dissolved in ½ cup water

Preheat oven to 350 ° F.

Core and cut apples into six pieces and boil in 8 cups of water for 15 to 20 minutes. Drain off all water, add remaining ingredients plus 2 cups of water. Stir it constantly over medium heat for 10 minutes. Roll pastry to fit bottom of pan, prick all sides with fork and add fruit mixture. Lattice the top with strips of pastry and bake for 1 hour or until golden brown. Serves 30-35.

Donald L. Dell

President, International Tennis Hall of Fame

LULLIE'S CUPBOARD

4 eggs, beaten
Scant ½ cup sugar
1 teaspoon vanilla
1 quart milk
Pinch of salt

Beat eggs, sugar and vanilla. Put milk in a double-boiler and heat slowly to room temperature, with a pinch of salt. Slowly add the egg mixture to the milk in the double-boiler. Cook slowly at a very low temperature. Stir constantly until your tablespoon is coated. (The trick is to remove the pan from the burner the instant the spoon coats.) Chill. If serving in small individual dishes, top with maraschino cherries or a dab of whipped cream. (Looks pretty served in stemmed glasses, too.) Also good over angel food or pound cake.

Julia Duffy

Actress

SORREL VEGETABLE SOUP

2 medium zucchini
3 tablespoons butter
1 clove garlic, minced
2 leeks sliced thin (white part only)
2 stalks celery, chopped
4 or 5 carrots, sliced
1 large onion, chopped
2 10-ounce cans chicken broth
½ cup chopped parsley
2 tablespoons tomato paste
½ cup chopped sorrel or to taste
½ cup cream

Slice zucchini and cook in small amount of water with salt until tender. Drain and puree in blender or food processor. Set aside.

Melt butter in large pan and saute leeks, carrots, onions, celery and garlic over medium heat about 10 minutes. Do not brown. Stir in tomato paste, zucchini puree, broth and parsley. Simmer just until vegetables are tender, about 20 minutes. Stir in cream and sorrel and heat for a few more minutes. About 4 first course servings.

Note. Sorrel can be found in better grocery stores and is easily grown. It looks like spinach but has a tangy, lemon taste.

Cliff Drysdale

Tennis Sportscaster

TERIYAKI SALMON

¼ cup soy sauce
2 tablespoons brown sugar
2 tablespoons fresh ginger, grated
1 pound salmon filets or steaks

Mix the soy sauce, sugar and ginger together in a plastic foodstorage bag. Marinate the salmon for 1 hour. Broil the salmon in the oven broiler or over charcoal. (10 minutes per inch of thickness for broiling time.)

Dick Enberg

Sportscaster

California Lemon Bread

½ cup butter
1 cup sugar
2 eggs
Grated zest of 1 large lemon
1½ cups flour
1 teaspoon baking powder
½ teaspoon salt
½ cup chopped pecans
½ cup milk
Lemon Glaze

Preheat oven to 350 ° F. Grease a 8" x 5" x 3" loaf pan and set aside.

In medium mixing bowl, cream butter and sugar. Beat in eggs thoroughly. In the following order, add lemon zest, flour, baking powder, salt, nuts and milk, continuing to mix until well blended. Pour batter into greased pans and bake until brown and toothpick inserted in center of loaves comes out clean, about 45 to 55 minutes (less time if you are making small loaves). Glaze over bread while still hot. Allow to cool in loaf pan.

Lemon Glaze

Juice of 1 lemon
½ cup sugar

Combine ingredients and mix well until sugar is completely dissolved.

Ken Farrar

Chief of Supervisors,
Men's Tennis Council

HOMEMADE VEGETABLE SOUP

Traveling on the tennis circuit as much as I do (26 - 30 weeks a year), one appreciates the finer cuisines around the world. However, to me, after all these fine dishes, my favorite is getting home and having my wife make one of her famous "homemade vegetable soups."

Unfortunately, there is no set recipe. She improvises with whatever is on hand – but she always starts with a chicken or turkey base. From there on it's a pinch of this, a pinch of that, and lots of vegetables along the lines of celery, cabbage, carrots, lettuce, potatoes, tomatoes, etc. There is nothing like a hot bowl of homemade soup! Not very glamorous – but that is my favorite recipe.

Steve Garvey

former infielder with the San Diego Padres

LAMB AND TRUFFLES

1 pound lamb shank
⅛ teaspoon ground saffron
1 14-ounce can white truffles, drained
¼ cup vegetable oil
1 cup water
1 clove garlic, chopped
1 dash salt
1 dash pepper

In a large saucepan, cover lamb with water. Add salt to taste, cover and simmer for one hour, or until meat is tender. Set aside. In skillet, combine oil, water, garlic, saffron and pepper to taste. Bring mixture to a boil; simmer 3 minutes. Drain meat and cut into bite-size pieces. Add to skillet mixture. Add truffles, cover and simmer 15 minutes.

Bob Graham

U. S. Senator from Florida

FLORIDA SEAFOOD CASSEROLE

½ **pound crab**
½ **pound Florida lobster**
1 **pound shrimp**
1 **cup mayonnaise**
½ **cup green pepper, chopped**
¼ **cup onion, minced**
1½ **cup celery, finely chopped**
½ **teaspoon salt**
1 **tablespoon Worcestershire sauce**
2 **cups crushed potato chips**
Paprika

Preheat oven to 400 ° F.

Mix all ingredients together, except chips and paprika. Fill a large baking pan
and cover completely with chips. Sprinkle with paprika. Bake for 20-25 minutes.
Serves 12.

Alexander Haig

former Secretary of State

HAWAIIAN CHICKEN

Use legs, thighs and breasts of 4 chickens

Preheat oven to 350 ° F.

In 3 tablespoons of fat, brown chicken. Remove and drain on paper towel.
Place in roasting pan with cover and cook about 1 hour, or until
tender.

Sweet and Sour Sauce:
2 cups brown sugar
2 cans pineapple chunks, drained and reserve juice equaling 1 ½ cups
4 tablespoons soy sauce
2 green peppers
¼ cup vinegar
2 tablespoons cornstarch
2 cans pineapple chunks, drained and juice reserved
1 can macadamia nuts, chopped (optional)

Cook all ingredients except pineapple chunks, green peppers and macadamia nuts. Stir this over medium heat until thickened and smooth. About 5 minutes before serving, add pineapple chunks and green peppers cut into comparable size (do not overcook). Place chicken on large platter, pour sauce over top and sprinkle macadamia nuts for garnish. (Sauce can be frozen). Serves 10.

Audrey Hepburn

Actress

YOGURT AND DILL SAUCE

(TO SERVE WITH COLD POACHED SALMON)

1 heaping tablespoon of mayonnaise
1 cup plain yogurt
Finely chopped fresh dill to taste

Thoroughly mix mayonnaise with yogurt, then add lots of the chopped dill. Spoon over salmon and sprinkle with more dill for garnish.

Gordie Howe

Hockey great

Beer Batter Fried Fish

2½ pound fillets - red snapper or flounder
½ inch thick Beer Batter:
    1 cup flour
    ½ teaspoon paprika
    ¼ teaspoon salt
    ⅛ teaspoon pepper
    ¾ cup beer
Salad oil, 2 inches deep in a skillet

Mix flour, paprika, salt and pepper. Slowly pour in beer. Beat until smooth. Dip fish into batter, drain. Cook a few pieces at a time, turning until golden brown (about 3-4 minutes in a deep fryer or deep pan filled with 2 inches of salad oil). Tastes nice with malt vinegar.

Hamilton Jordan

former Chief Executive, Association of Tennis Professionals

Oriental Sesame Chicken

4 (8 ounces each) chicken breasts (skinned and boneless)
1 4-ounce bottle Oriental oyster sauce
1 bunch fresh broccoli, cut into florets
2 ounces Oriental teriyaki sauce
1 medium size onion, cut into strips
2 ounces of water
1 tablespoon garlic, minced
2 ounces sesame oil
1 tablespoon cornstarch, dissolved in cold water
3 tablespoons sesame seeds (heaping)
No salt

Cut the chicken breasts into strips about 2 inches long and ½ inch wide and place to the side. Peel onion and cut into strips about ¼ inch wide. Cut broccoli into nice florets.

Add sesame oil to a large saute pan, wok or iron skillet, and put on medium heat. When oil is fairly hot, add onion and sesame seeds to the pan. Saute until sesame seeds turn golden brown. Add chicken and saute until almost completely cooked then add oyster sauce, teriyaki sauce and water and continue to cook.

When the liquid begins to boil, add the cornstarch mixture until it thickens. At this point, fold the broccoli and onions into the mixture. Cover and cook only 5-8 minutes so the broccoli and onions are still crunchy. Serves 8.

Rich Kaufman

ATP Chair Umpire

GRILLED SALMON

Soy sauce or teriyaki sauce (enough to cover the surface of a shallow baking pan)
½ teaspoon garlic, minced
Salmon steaks
Ginger
Black pepper
Any other favorite spices

Blend garlic with sauce. Place steaks in the pan and marinate on each side for 5 minutes. Remove from the pan and place on a large piece of foil. The foil will protect the steaks while they are cooking and prevent them from breaking apart on the grill.

Sprinkle ginger, black pepper, and any other favorite spices on the steaks. Place a small piece of butter on top of the fish and close foil. Use a fork to make small holes on top of the foil for heat to come through. Place on a hot grill and cook until the meat is a light pink color. It does not need to be turned during cooking. When salmon is almost done, pour some of the sauce over the fish, reclose the foil and finish cooking.

This goes well with baked sweet potatoes and any green vegetable in season. It also goes well with bagels and cream cheese for breakfast.

Edward M. Kennedy

U. S. Senator from Massachussetts

CAPE COD FISH CHOWDER

2 pounds fresh haddock
2 ounces salt pork, diced
2 medium onions, sliced
1 cup chopped celery
4 large potatoes, diced
1 bay leaf, crumbled
4 cups milk
2 tablespoons butter or margarine
1 teaspoon salt
Freshly ground black pepper to taste

Simmer haddock in 2 cups of water for 15 minutes. Drain off and reserve the broth. Remove the skin and bones from the fish. Saute the diced salt pork in a large pot until crisp. Remove salt pork and saute onions in the pork fat until golden brown.

Add fish, celery, potatoes and bay leaf. Measure reserved fish broth, plus enough boiling water, to make 3 cups liquid. Add to pot and simmer 30 minutes. Add milk and butter and simmer for an additional 5 minutes, or until well heated. Season with salt and pepper. Makes 8 servings.

Knott's Berry Farm

STRAWBERRY WALDORF MOLD

16 ounce box red raspberry gelatin
1½ cups boiling water
2 cups ice water
1 8-ounce package cream cheese, softened
1 cup sour cream
½ cup Knott's Berry Farm Strawberry Preserves

1 teaspoon lemon juice
½ cup apple, chopped
½ cup walnuts, chopped
½ cup celery, chopped (optional)

In medium bowl, combine gelatin and boiling water and mix until gelatin is dissolved. Stir in ice water and set aside. In large bowl, whip cream cheese. Add sour cream, preserves and lemon juice. Beat on low speed until creamy. Slowly pour gelatin into cream cheese mixture while continuing to beat until well blended. Stir in apples, walnuts and celery and pour into 2 quart mold. Refrigerate at least 6 hours.

To unmold, dip mold just to rim in warm water about 10 seconds. Shake to loosen. Top with wet plate. Invert plate and mold together, remove lid. Makes 8 to 10 servings.

Bernie Kopell

Actor

BURRO SHEETOE

4 cooked large chicken breasts, boned, skinned and cut into bite size
    chunks*
2 cups bean sprouts
2 cups celery, chopped
¾ cup raw sunflower seeds
Cheddar cheese, sliced
Mayonnaise to bind
Salt and pepper to taste
Curry, enough to sprinkle on top

Preheat oven to 350 ° F.

Fold together chicken, sprouts, celery, sunflower seeeds and mayonnaise. Add salt and pepper to taste. Put in flat casserole dish and cover with cheese. Bake in oven until heated.

*Can substitute equal amount of turkey breast.

Bowie Kuhn

former Commissioner of Baseball

A southern dish from Bowie's Maryland backround.

Spoon Bread

1 cup water, boiling
½ cup white cornmeal
½ cup milk
1½ teaspoons baking powder
1 tablespoon butter, softened
2 eggs, well beaten

Prehat oven to 400 ° F. Butter a 1 quart casserole or baking dish.

Pour water over corn meal. Beat in milk, baking powder and butter. Add eggs. Dry ingredients may be mixed in advance, then add water, milk and eggs. Pour into casserole or baking dish, and bake for 20 to 25 minutes until set and serve immediately. May be multiplied.

Delicious with roast chicken and gravy. Serves 3 (or 4 small eaters).

Larry, Darryl and Darryl

Actors

This was our Granddad's favorite wartime recipe, taken right from Grandma's recipe book dated 1927. Darryl says he is proud to pass on such an Epicurean delight. Bon appetite!

ROAST SQUIRRELS

Squirrels
Salad oil
Lemon juice or tarragon vinegar
1 cup breadcrumbs
Cream
1 cup button mushrooms
Pepper and salt
Onion juice
Oil
Brown stock
Worcestershire sauce
Paprika

Clean the squirrels thoroughly, wash in several waters and cover with salad oil mixed with lemon juice or tarragon vinegar. Let stand for an hour on a platter. Soak a cup of breadcrumbs in just enough cream to moisten them, add a cup of button mushrooms and dice, then add pepper, salt and onion juice. Stuff each squirrel with this mixture, sew and truss as you would fowl. Rub with oil, place in a dripping-dish, and partly cover with brown stock diluted with a cup of boiling water. When the squirrels are well roasted, make a gravy out of the liquid in the pan, by adding a teaspoon of Worcestershire sauce and paprika, salt and lemon juice to taste.

Robin Leach

Television Personality

REALLY RICH AND EXPENSIVE CHICKEN *(BUT WELL WORTH IT)*

**1 whole chicken cut up into breasts, wings and legs or chicken
    parts you prefer**
Sliced onions
1 can petit pois peas (not warehouse brand peas)
1 can mushroom soup
Butter
1 can baby carrots (again not warehouse brand carrots)
Basil and oregano
Black pepper
5 small potatoes, peeled
**Champagne (the more expensive the label e.g. Kristal or Dom Perignon-
    the better the taste of the final cooked dish)**

Preheat oven to 425 ° F (475 ° F if using a Romertopf casserole).

Wash and dry the chicken. Heavily scatter spices, flavorings or your choice such
as Lea and Perrins sauce, powdered mustard, squeezed lemon juice etc. on the
chicken topping it off with slices of butter, which should hold spices to the
chicken skin. If using a Romertopf pot soak in cold water for 20 minutes. If
using a Pyrex or similar dish use in normal way.

Then place generous quantities of sliced onions on bottom of pot. Pour in a
dribble of champagne. Then place chicken on top. Pour in another dribble of
champagne. Then place peas on top. Add your choice of herbs or spices and
pour in another dribble of champagne. Then place carrots on top. Again add
your choice of herbs or spices, three slices of butter placed at even distance
over the carrots and add a double-dribble of champagne. Smooth the mushroom
soup (uncooked) as a paste over all of this. Sink the peeled potatoes into the
mushroom soup-covered vegetables. Leave top half of potatoes exposed. Pour
in sufficient champagne so liquid is level to the covered vegetables. Place in
oven and cook for one hour with lid on. After that one hour remove lid and
continue to bake for approximately 15 minutes to brown the exposed half of the
potatoes. Remove from oven, eat, enjoy and be merry. Your dinner guests will
praise you and you'll modestly admit you can't pass on the recipe because you
stole it from the Rockefellers!

Left: Horseshoe Piazza at International Tennis Hall of Fame
Photo by Michael Baz

Rich Little

Comedian

CHICKEN LITTLE

6 boneless chicken breasts skinned
Butter
Flour
1 small carton whipping cream
Grated parmesan cheese
1 cup fresh mushrooms

Preheat oven to 350° F.

Dip chicken breasts in melted butter then in flour. Place chicken in an oven-proof dish just big enough to fit the breasts in a single layer. Pour whipping cream over chicken (just enough to cover chicken). Sprinkle parmesan over chicken. Slice mushrooms and put over top of cheese. Bake for 30 to 40 minutes.

Harvey Mackay

Author of Swim With The Sharks

PECAN PIE

1 pie shell
3 to 4 eggs whipped with a fork (3 extra large, or 4 large)
½ cup sugar
Dash salt
¼ teaspoon cornstarch
1 teaspoon vanilla
1 cup dark corn syrup
1½ - 2 cups pecans
4 tablespoons butter

Preheat oven to 450 ° F.

The pie shell is always made with shortening which is cut into the flour.

Mix sugar, salt, cornstarch together and pour into eggs, beat and mix very well. Mix vanilla and syrup together. Pour pecans into mixture and mix. Put all in pie shell and dot with butter. Bake for 10 to 15 minutes, then reduce oven to 350 ° F and continue baking for an additional 35 minutes. (Pie is done when blade ofknife is inserted and comes out clean.)

Ron Machtley

Congressman from Rhode Island

LOBSTER THERMIDOR

2 boiled lobsters
¼ pound fresh mushrooms
2 tablespoons butter
2 ounces sherry or cooking wine (optional)
2 tablespoons flour
1 cup milk or cream
¼ cup diced cheddar cheese
Paprika
2 egg yolks

Boil lobsters and remove meat. Reserve shells. Saute lobster meat and sliced mushrooms in butter for 5 minutes. Add salt and pepper to taste. Add sherry and braise for 2 minutes. Blend flour into mixture, then slowly stir in milk. Add cheese and stir until it melts. Sprinkle with paprika. Remove from heat and blend in egg yolks. Fill lobster shells. Sprinkle with parmesan cheese and a dash of paprika. Place under broiler to brown.

Dina Merrill

Actress

Ceviche

½ pound bay scallops
½ pound white fish (bass, grouper or cod), cut into small pieces
Juice of one lemon
½ cup sweet onion
½ cup green pepper, diced
½ cup tomato, diced
Cilantro

Marinate seafood in lemon juice overnight. Drain and mix with sweet onion, peppers and tomatoes and add cilantro. Serve as first course, chilled.

Arthur Murray

Father of American Ballroom Dancing

"For years I kept trying to equal a cake that Arthur remembered from his childhood. With each try, I jotted down my experimental measurements. Finally, Arthur tasted it and said, 'This is better than my mother's, I've never changed the recipe since then."

Kathryn Murray's Honey Cake

4 eggs at room temperature
¼ teaspoon salt
6 tablespoons sweet butter
½ cup granulated sugar
¾ cup honey (I prefer orange blossom)
2 cups cake flour
1½ teaspoon baking powder
¼ teaspoon baking soda
4 tablespoons instant coffee (powdered variety; if not available, use ¼
     cup of very strong coffee, cooled)

1 large navel orange rind, grated
1 cup walnut pieces, cut, not chopped

Preheat oven to 325 ° F. Use large open roasting pan, about 10" x 15". Butter it lightly, then flour the pan, shaking out the excess flour by tapping the pan over the sink.

Cream butter, gradually, until well blended. Fold in sugar until blended. Sift flour, baking powder, baking soda and coffee. Fold in sifted ingredients, which can be added all at once.

Fold thoroughly until no specks of flour show. Fold in the orange rind and the cut nuts and blend well. Spread evenly in the prepared baking pan and bake in the preheated oven for 35 to 45 minutes until the cake has medium brown edges and has separated from the sides of the pan. Place in tightly covered cookie tin, use wax paper between layers. All honey cakes taste better a few days after baking. This cake keeps very well.

Bob Newhart

Actor

IRISH COLCANNON

1½ pounds potatoes
1½ cups milk
6 chopped scallions
1½ cups boiled cabbage
1 tablespoon butter
1 tablespoon parsley, chopped
Salt and pepper to taste

Boil and mash potatoes. Boil the milk and add to potatoes. Next add the chopped scallions and beat until fluffy. Finely chop the cooked cabbage and add it with melted butter tossing carefully. Finally add the parsley, salt and pepper and fold well. This is as Irish as Soda Bread.

Paul Newman

Actor

CHICKEN CREOLE

1 medium onion, chopped
1 green pepper, chopped
1 tablespoon vegetable oil
2 cups diced cooked chicken
1 cup cooked rice
2 cups Newman's Own spaghetti sauce
Dash ground nutmeg

Saute onion and pepper in oil until limp. Add chicken, rice, spaghetti sauce, and nutmeg. Simmer, covered, over low heat for 45 minutes or bake at 350 ° F for 45 minutes. Serves 4-5.

Thomas P. O'Neill, Jr.

former Speaker of The U. S. House of Representatives

BEER ROAST

4 pound beef roast (round, rump or sirloin)
Salt and pepper
½ cup sugar
1 small bottle catsup
2 cans beer
4 medium carrots (¼ inch slices)
2 medium onions, sliced
1 large green pepper, diced coarse
2 large stalks celery, sliced
Cooked rice or noodles

Preheat oven to 350 ° F.

Place roast in open pan, season with salt and pepper and bake for ½ hours. Combine sugar, catsup and beer and add to meat with vegetables. Reduce oven heat to 325° F and cook uncovered until tender. Delicious served with rice or egg noodles. Serves 12-16. May be frozen.

Bobby Orr

former Hockey great and Hall of Famer

Pasta Salad

Dressing:
¾ cup olive oil
2½ tablespoons red wine vinegar
Juice of one lemon
1 large garlic clove, minced
1 tablespoon fresh dill, minced
1 tablespoon fresh basil, minced
1 tablespoon fresh parsley, minced
2 tablespoons Dijon mustard
2 tablespoons honey
½ teaspoon salt
Freshly ground pepper

Blend all ingredients in food processor or blender. Let sit in refrigerator for at least several hours.

Salad:
18 ounces of pasta shells, rotini, or whatever shape you like
4 scallions, chopped
1½ cup ham, cut in strips
¾ cup thawed peas
1 cup Swiss cheese, cut in strips
1 green bell pepper, cut in thin strips
½ red bell, cut in strips

Cook pasta until "al dente" and cool. Add remaining ingredients and toss. Add dressing, mix in thoroughly (chill if desired) and serve.

Tom Poston

Actor

KENNEBUNK PICKLE

2 pounds fresh green tomatoes
2 pounds fresh red tomatoes
1 small head of cabbage
2 sweet red peppers
2 green peppers
¾ quart onions, optional
1 bunch celery
6 tablespoons salt
1 quart white vinegar
3 cups brown sugar
1 3-inch cinnamon stick
1 teaspoon whole cloves
1 teaspoon dry mustard

Chop vegetables very fine. Add salt and let stand ovemight. Drain. Add vinegar and brown sugar. Tie cinnamon, cloves and mustard in a small cheesecloth bag. Boil everything together for about 30 minutes. Remove cheesecloth bag. Pour into sterilized jars and seal. Makes 5 quarts pickle. A very old recipe that goes good with a glass of iced tea and a midsummer's night on an old front porch.

Wolfgang Puck

Owner/Chef, Spago Restaurant

CRABCAKES WITH SWEET RED PEPPER

½ red onion
2 red peppers
2 cups of sweet cream
¼ jalapeno or cayenne
1 pound crabmeat, (Louisiana blue crab)
½ pound bread crumbs
1 bunch chives, chopped
½ cup onions, chopped

4 cloves garlic, chopped
½ teaspoon basil, or thyme
½ cup white wine
¼ sweet butter
salt and pepper to taste
½ lemon
olive oil
balsamic vinegar
1 pound arugula

Saute diced onions and one red pepper. Cool. Reduce half of the cream with the jalapeno. Let cool. When everything is cold, mix crabmeat with 2 tablespoons bread crumbs, chives, reduced cream and onion-pepper mixture. Form 12 small round cakes and bread them with remaining crumbs. Reserve until needed. In saucepan, saute onions with the remaining pepper, the garlic and thyme (or basil). Deglaze with white wine, reduce. Add cream, bring to a boil and puree in electric blender until smooth. Add butter, salt and pepper and the juice of ½ lemon. Strain and keep warm. Saute crabcakes in oil and butter for about 4 minutes on each side. Remove to a paper towel to drain. Mix olive oil with a little balsamic vinegar, salt and pepper. Add to the arugula salad. Place and put crabcakes on top.

Renee Richards, M.D.

former tennis professional and tennis coach

Boston Baked Beans

2 cups dried navy beans
½ pound salt pork, halved
½ cup dark molasses
2 teaspoons grated onion
½ teaspoon dry mustard

Soak beans overnight in water to cover. Bring to a boil in the same water, reduce heat, cover and simmer for 1 hour. Drain, save water.

Preheat oven to 300 ° F.

Put half of pork in 6 cup bean pot. Add beans, molasses, onion, mustard and ½ cup bean water. Put other half of pork on top. Cover and bake in oven for 5 hours, add more bean water if needed. Uncover, bake for 1 hour. Serves 6.

Kenny Rogers

Actor and singer

Chicken Salad a la Rogers

2 cups cooked chicken (white meat)
3 dill pickles (non-Kosher), skinned
½ cup walnuts, chopped
¼ cup almonds, slivered or chopped

Pick the chicken from the bone rather than cut it. Peel pickles with a potato peeler and chop. Mix all of the above ingredients lightly with dressing of your choice. You may prefer to add chopped scallions. Season to taste and serve on a bed of crisp lettuce.

Susan Ruttan

Actress

Surprise Chicken Chili

6 tablespoons olive oil
1 onion, chopped (about 1 cup)
5 cloves garlic, minced
2 sweet red peppers, diced (about 2 cups)
2 to 4 jalapeno peppers, seeds removed, minced
2 to 3 tablespoons chili pepper
1 tablespoon ground cinnamon
1 ½ teaspoons ground cumin
1 teaspoon ground coriander
6 skinless, boneless chicken breast halves, cubed
1 15-ounce can tomato puree
1 16-ounce can pitted black olives, drained and sliced
1 cup beer or chicken broth
¼ cup unsweetened chocolate, grated
¼ cup Monterey Jack or Cheddar cheese
1 avocado, chopped
Sour cream

Heat half the olive oil in a large saucepan or Dutch oven over medium-high heat. Add onion and garlic. Saute 2 to 3 minutes, stirring frequently. Add both kinds of peppers and continue to saute and stir for 10 minutes. Add chili powder, cinnamon, cumin and coriander. Stir and reduce heat. While vegetables simmer, heat remaining oil in 12-inch skillet over medium-high heat. Add chicken and cook quickly, stirring frequently until chicken turns white. Using slotted spoon, transfer to a saucepan with vegetables. Add tomato puree, olives and beer or broth. Add grated chocolate and mix well. Simmer over low heat for 15 to 20 minutes more, stirring occasionally. Serve garnished with grated cheese, chopped avocado and sour cream. Makes 6 servings.

George Schultz

former Secretary of State

FIREPLACE SIRLOIN

2½ inch thick sirloin steak (3 to 4 pounds)
Table salt

Before cooking, fireplace should be in use for about 3 hours, providing a deep, hot bed of wood ashes. When ready to cook the steak, remove some of the hot embers from the burning logs and place the logs to the side of the fire (remaining embers will be used to cook the second side of the steak).

Pour salt over one side of the steak until it is completely covered. Place the steak, salt side down, on the hot embers. Cook about 25 minutes. Remove steak from the embers and brush off the remaining salt.

Stir embers and add remaining embers from the logs that have been set aside. Salt the uncooked side of the steak and place, salt side down, on the embers. Cook about 20 minutes for rare. Remove from embers, brush off remaining salt. Place on platter and carve in thin slices.

Dip slices in melted butter and place on bread. You may want to serve this with a large green salad.

This is a great way to entertain six people infomally.

Eugene Scott

Editor of Tennis Week

My recipe is more attitude than ingredients. For years I have heard women (more recently men) decry how they spend hours slaving over a hot stove to prepare a single meal. Frankly I don't see the sense in all the anguish. My recipe, therefore, above all else, is for simplicity.

First buy the best wine and champagne your budget can afford. Maybe more than you can afford. The guests will be so dazzled (and plastered) by your high style that by the time the soup course is done they couldn't care less whether the cuisine is haute or hot. By the way, I would buy the soup from a club nearby. Club cooking usually is awful except for the soup. Follow soup with Chicken Tarragon - a four pound broiler enough for 4 people. Ask the butcher to pre-cut the chicken into 7 pieces, separate the legs from the second joint to prevent the messy process of dishevelment (sometimes called carving) at the table. Sprinkle tarragon seasoning liberally, put in a pyrex dish and pop in a 400° F oven for 40 minutes. Baked potatoes and broccoli are a cinch in the microwave, and anyone with the IQ of a warm plate can make a good salad.

For dessert? Instead of Cherries Jubilee, I prefer my own concoction - Grapes Jubilee. White grapes, vanilla Haagen Dazs and a splash of brown sugar in your best silver tennis bowl on which your name is engraved in large enough letters for the guests to ogle. Follow with coffee and enough fine brandy that by morning the guests will neither know what they had for dinner nor where they had it.

Roger Staubach

former Dallas Cowboy quarterback and Hall of Famer

ORANGE HONEY CHICKEN AND RICE

6 ounces orange juice concentrate
1 stick of margarine
4 tablespoons honey
4 to 6 chicken breast halves

Preheat oven to 350 ° F.

Heat together, juice, margarine and honey. Place chicken in a Pyrex dish. Pour all of the sauce except ½ cup, over chicken and bake 45 minutes to 1 hour.

Prepare Uncle Ben's Brown and Wild Rice according to package directions and add the ½ cup of remaining sauce, plus ½ cup chopped pecans.

Put rice on platter and place chicken on top and pour any remaining sauce over it and serve.

Connie Stevens

Singer

CRANBERRY MOLD

2 boxes strawberry jello (large)
2 15-ounce cans whole cranberries
2 apples (large), peeled and grated on long side of grater
12 ounces walnuts, chopped
7½ cups water

Dissolve jello in 5 cups of boiling water. Add 2 cans of whole cranberries. Add apple and walnuts. Add remaining water. Mold and refrigerate. When ready to serve, unmold and sprinkle with walnuts on top.

Betty Stove
Tennis Coach

ASPARAGUS WITH PARMESAN CHEESE

2 pounds of asparagus (fresh)
½ teaspoon salt
⅔ cup parmesan cheese (fresh)
5 tablespoons butter

Preheat oven to 450 ° F. Butter a bake-and-serve dish.

Boil the asparagus for 5 minutes. Lay the asparagus row by row, never covering the tip. Spread each layer with salt and cheese and a bit of butter before putting on the next layer of asparagus. Bake for 15 minutes until crust is golden brown. Take it out of the oven to settle for a few minutes and serve with a nice cooled white wine. A great appetizer. Serves 4 people.

Bill Toomey
1968 U. S. Olympic Gold Medal winner in the Decathalon

CHICKEN BREAST BEAUREGARD

4 ounces clarifed butter
1 6-ounce chicken breast, skinned and boned
1 clove garlic, finely chopped
1 shallot, finely chopped
3 each mushrooms
2 ounces white wine
6 each raw shrimp, cut up
6 each oysters, cut up
2 tablespoons fresh bread crumbs
Salt and pepper to taste
3 ounces bearnaise sauce

Saute chicken in 2 ounces butter until done. While chicken cooks, in a separate pan, heat remaining butter. Saute garlic, shallot, mushrooms and wine very lightly. Add shrimp, oysters, bread crumbs, salt and pepper. Saute about 2 minutes. Spoon over chicken breast and top with bearnaise sauce. Serves 1.

Roy T. Van Brundt

National Chairman of Umpires USTA

Serves a mixed doubles match

Breast of Tennis Chicken - a confection of the rules

Ingredients (and permanent fixtures):
2 whole chicken breasts, skinned, boned and halved
¼ cup flour
1 tablespoon butter for each player (4)
1 tablespoon oil
3 tablespoons lemon juice
3 tablespoons parsley, minced
4 thin slices of lemon

Procedures:
Take up a ready position, and flatten the breast halves with a 4 ⅝" racquet handle, wrapped in wax paper, using a western grip. Drop shot the flour lightly onto each breast (of the chicken) in a skillet. Heat the 4 tablespoons of butter during the first half of the allowable warm-up period (5 minutes). You may practice some forehand and backhand volleys while waiting. Suggest not trying overheads or service in the kitchen.

When hot and foaming (the chicken, not you!), saute for the remainder of the warm-up period plus the 30 seconds allowed for first serve (2.5 to 3 minutes) on deuce side, then turn over and repeat the procedure ("second serve") on the ad side, until nicely brown. Remove and keep warm, allowing for continuous play as provided by Rule 30.

Add salt and pepper and lemon juice to skillet, stir, deglaze, and remove all brown particles. "Ad" remaining butter and parsley to skillet, blend, return the breasts to pan, and re-warmup - the chicken - (for one minute).

Place meat on first service platter with forehand stroke. Spoon pan juices over it, using slice backhand. Delicately drop shot a lemon slice on each piece at match point.

Line umpires ready? Players ready? "Serve" with a dry French wine available at your local Roland Garros.

Dionne Warwick

Singer

Chicken and Dumplings

1 4 ½ to 5 pound stewing chicken, cut up
1 medium onion, studded with 3 whole cloves
3 celery tops
1 carrot, sliced
2 bay leaves
1 tablespoon salt
3 cups hot water
1 ⅓ cups all-purpose flour
2 teaspoons double-acting baking powder
1 teaspoon parsley, chopped
½ teaspoon salt
3 cups milk
2 tablespoons salad oil

Place chicken, onion, celery, carrot, bay leaves, and salt in 8-quart saucepan. Add hot water and heat to boiling over high heat. Cover and simmer 2 to 2 $^{1}/_{2}$ hours. Discard onion, celery and bay leaves.

In large bowl, stir flour, baking powder, parsley and salt, with a fork. In cup, combine milk and salad oil. Slowly stir into flour until soft dough forms. Drop by heaping tablespoons onto chicken. Cook uncovered 10 minutes, cover and cook 10 minutes more. With slotted spoon, remove dumplings. Spoon chicken into serving dish and top with dumplings.

Right: The cupola of the
International Tennis Hall of Fame
Newport, R.I.

Wilhelm Wachtmeister

former Senior Swedish Ambassador to the U. S.

GRANDMOTHER'S PANCAKES

100 grams butter
100 grams all-purpose flour
1 cup water, boiled
1 cup heavy cream
6 eggs yolks
6 egg whites, whipped
butter for coating pan

Mix butter and flour with boiling water. After cooling off a bit, mix in the egg yolks, then the cream. Add the whipped egg whites. Bake on top of the stove slowly and lightly in butter in an ordinary pancake iron. Bake only on one side.

Layer pancakes with a thick vanilla cream or custard between each layer (raspberry jam could also be used). Put a layer of sugar on top of cake and make a pattern with a hot iron.

Serve cake warm with fresh berries. The cake could be made in advance and heated up.

'Coach' Charleye Wright

Sportscaster, Los Angleles, CA

KEEP YOUR EYE ON THE COACH CANDY

1 cup butter or margarine, softened
2½ cups flour
2 cups brown sugar
2 eggs
4 teaspoons vanilla
1 teaspoon soda
3 cups quick-cooking rolled oats
1½ cups semisweet chocolate pieces
1 can (1¼ cups) sweetened condensed milk

2 tablespoons margarine or butter
½ cup walnuts, chopped

Preheat oven to 350 ° F. Line a 15" x 10" x 1" baking pan with foil.

In large mixer bowl, beat 1 cup of butter with electric mixer. Add half the flour, all the brown sugar, eggs, 2 teaspoons of vanilla and soda. Beat on low and add remaining flour and oats, stir.

In medium saucepan, cook chocolate pieces, condensed milk and 2 tablespoons butter on low heat. Remove, and stir in remaining vanilla and nuts. Pat   ⅔ of oat mixture (3½ cups) into bottom of prepared pan. Spread chocolate mixture over oat mixture. Dot with remaining oat mixture. Bake for 25 minutes. Cool and cut into bars.

Glenn William

Tennis Coach

Fettuccine with Bacon, Mushrooms, and Sundried Tomatoes

2 quarts fresh mushrooms
¼ stick butter
4 cloves garlic
3 cups of sundried tomatoes
¾ cup of olive oil
1 pound of bacon
2 pounds fresh fettuccine
1½ cups parmesan cheese, finely grated
Freshly ground white and black pepper
1 bunch of scallions, thinly chopped

Slice mushrooms in half and saute in a large skillet with butter over high heat until crisp. Crush cloves of garlic and add to mushrooms. Add sundried tomatoes and ¼ cup of oil to mushrooms in skillet. Chop bacon and crisp over high heat. Drain fat. Then add to ingredients in skillet. Simmer over low heat.

Boil fettuccine for 2 minutes. Drain and empty into a large shallow bowl. Thoroughly toss with ½ cup of olive oil and parmesan cheese. Add the mushrooms, sundried tomatoes, bacon and garlic from the skillet and toss. Pepper to taste. Garnish on top with scallions.

Barry Williams

Director of "Pretty Woman"

CREAMY APRICOT CHICKEN

1 teaspoon each of margarine and olive oil or vegetable oil
2 chicken cutlets (¼ pound each), pounded to ¼-inch thickness
1 tablespoon shallot, chopped
1 tablespoon all-purpose flour
¼ cup sweet vermouth
½ cup canned chicken broth
1 tablespoon non-fat plain yogurt
8 dried apricot halves, blanched
1 teaspoon fresh Italian (flat leaf) parsley, chopped

In skillet combine margarine and oil, heat until margarine is melted. Add chicken and cook, turning once, until both sides are browned and chicken is cooked through, 2 to 3 minutes on each side. Remove chicken from skillet and set aside and keep warm.

To same skillet add shallot and saute over medium heat until softened, about one minute. Sprinkle flour over shallot and stir quickly to combine. Cook, stirring constantly, for 1 minute. Continuing to stir, gradually add vermouth and stir in broth and cook over low heat until mixture is slightly thickened, 4 to 5 minutes. Stir in yogurt.

To serve, arrange chicken on serving platter, top with sauce and apricot halves and sprinkle with parsley.

TENNIS PARTIES

*W*e compiled
this chapter with the
professional help of Martha Stewart
and Plantation Catering --
an exceptional caterer based in
Newport, Rhode Island. With these
menu suggestions and
recipes you will be able to entertain
around your tennis afternoons and
the numerous televised tennis
broadcasts, especially the
Grand Slam Events.

Preceding page: Lawn Tennis Championship
of the State of Pennsylvania trophy
Men's Singles
Photo by John Hopf

TENNIS MENU

Martha Stewart

Buttermilk-Potato Soup

Frittata

Bruschette

Berries with Framboise

Buttermilk-Potato Soup

8 small yellow Finnish potatoes or 12 tiny red new potatoes
2 tablespoons unsalted butter
2 tablespoons olive oil
1 large garlic clove, finely minced
3 large Vidalia onions, coarsely chopped
1 yellow bell pepper, finely julienned
½ pound large shrimp, peeled and deveined
1 Kirby cucumber, peeled, seeded, and slivered crosswise
2 tablespoons chopped fresh chives
2 teaspoons chopped fresh tarragon
1½ quarts buttermilk, cold from the refrigerator
salt and freshly ground pepper

Leaving the skins on, cook the potatoes in simmering water until tender,
15 or 20 minutes. Drain and set aside.

Meanwhile, melt the butter with the oil in a heavy skillet and saute garlic,
onion and pepper for about 15 minutes. Add the shrimp and continue to
saute just until the shrimp is cooked, about 5 more minutes.

To serve, quarter the potatoes and divide among 4 large, shallow soup
platters. Distribute the sauteed garlic, onion, pepper, and shrimp evenly
over the potatoes. Add the slivered cucumber, chives, and tarragon. Pour in
the buttermilk and season to taste with salt and pepper, stirring gently.
Serves 4 to 6.

Frittata

½ **cup olive oil**
9 eggs, lightly beaten
salt and freshly ground pepper

Topping 1:
4 cloves garlic, peeled and minced
1 small bunch broccoli rabe, coarsely chopped
½ **cup fresh porcini mushrooms, cleaned and thinly sliced**

Topping 2:
3 scallions, trimmed and thinly sliced
6 yellow cherry tomatoes, thinly sliced
10-12 fresh sage leaves

Heat all but about 3 tablespoons of the olive oil in a heavy 10-inch skillet. Pour the eggs into the hot pan and cook over medium-low heat for 4 to 6 minutes, drawing the eggs away from the sides of the pan with a fork or small spatula so that the uncooked eggs run to the sides and cook.

Spread the topping of your choice on the eggs and cook 2-4 minutes longer.

Heat the remaining oil in a 12-inch skillet. Carefully loosen the frittata from its smaller pan and flip it into the larger one, top side down. Cook 3-4 minutes, making sure the eggs are cooked through. Carefully invert the frittata onto a warm platter, season with salt and pepper, and serve immediately.

Bruschette

1 loaf crusty Italian bread
2 large cloves garlic, sliced in half
½ cup extra virgin olive oil
Kosher salt

Slice bread diagonally into 1-inch thick slices.

Arrange bread on a baking sheet and place under a broiler until the edges are golden brown but center is still soft.

Rub the slices with the garlic and, using a pastry brush, brush with ½ of the olive oil.

Sprinkle lightly with Kosher salt.

Turn slices over and place under broiler again. Rub the other side with garlic, brush with remaining olive oil, and sprinkle with Kosher salt. Serve immediately.

Berries with Framboise

1 pint ripe red raspberries
½ pint ripe blackberries
½ pint blueberries
1 tablespoon framboise (raspberry liqueur)

Gently toss the berries together in a serving bowl.

Sprinkle with the liqueur and serve. Serves 4 to 6.

COURT SIDE MENU

Plantation Catering
Newport, Rhode Island

SWEET AND SOUR LEEKS

WHITE BEAN SALAD WITH
TOMATOES AND OLIVES

MARINATED SEAFOOD AND
BLOOD ORANGE SALAD

SHORTBREAD SANDWICH COOKIES

Sweet and Sour Leeks

2 bunched leeks, trimmed and cleaned
2 tablespoons pine nuts
¼ cup olive oil
1 tablespoon currants
10 plum tomatoes, peeled, seeded, coarsely chopped
¼ cup red wine vinegar
2 tablespoons brown sugar
Coarse salt to taste

Saute pine nuts in 2 tablespoons of the olive oil in large saute pan. When they begin to color, add currants and tomatoes and saute 2 minutes. Add the leeks and remaining oil and enough water to cover leeks. Simmer partially covered for 15 minutes, or until tender. Remove the leeks to serving dish. Turn heat to high and reduce the juices. Add vinegar and sugar to pan and salt to taste. Reduce until sauce has body, taste to correct sweet and sour as needed.

White Bean Salad

2 cups cooked white beans
¼ cup olive oil
Salt and pepper to taste
2 large tomatoes, peeled, seeded and diced
¼ cup diced red onion
2 tablespoons fresh oregano, chopped or 2 teaspoons dried
¼ cup black olives, chopped

Toss ingredients together and taste for seasonings.

Right: Lantern and ivy at the
International Tennis Hall of Fane
Newport, R.I.
Photo courtesy of the International Tennis Hall of Fame

Marinated Seafood and Blood Orange Salad

3 2½-inch strips of blood orange rind, removed with a vegetable peeler
2½ x 2½ inch strip of lemon rind, removed with a vegetable peeler
12 coriander sprigs
2 quarter size slices of fresh gingerroot
6 black peppercorns
½ teaspoon salt
¾ pound large shrimp, shelled and deveined
¾ pound sea scallops, halved horizontally, if large
3 blood oranges plus ¼ cup blood orange juice
¼ cup fresh lime juice

Maltaise mayonnaise:
1 tablespoon blood orange juice
1 tablespoon fresh lime juice
1 large egg yolk
1 teaspoon Dijon style mustard
¼ teaspoon minced garlic if desired
¼ teaspoon crushed fresh gingerroot (forced through a garlic press)
¼ cup vegetable oil
¼ cup olive oil
½ cup minced red or green bell pepper
⅓ cup minced red onion or scallion
⅓ cup minced fresh coriander plus additional whole leaves for garnish

Red leaf lettuce leaves for lining the platter

In a saucepan, combine orange and lemon rind, coriander sprigs, gingerroot, peppercorns and salt with 3 cups of water, bring to a boil, and simmer the mixture for 15 minutes. Let the mixture cool to room temperature and strain it through a sieve into a saucepan. Add shrimp and scallops, and bring liquid to a simmer. Stir and drain the seafood in a colander. In a bowl, combine the orange juice and the lime juice and the seafood, let it marinate, covered loosely, stirring occasionally to coat it with the marinade for 3 hours.

Using a zester or the fine side of a grater, grate the rind from 2 oranges, keeping it in long shreds. Reserve it, wrapped in a dampened paper towel. With a serrated knife, cut away the pith from 2 oranges and cut away the rind and the pith from the remaining orange. Cut the oranges crosswise into thin slices and re-

Marinated Seafood and Blood Orange Salad (continued)

serve them, covered and chilled.

Make the Maltaise mayonnaise in a food processor or blender. Blend together the orange juice, lime juice, yolk, mustard, garlic, gingerroot, salt and pepper to taste. With the motor running, add the oils in a stream and blend the mayonnaise until it is emulsified.

In a bowl, combine the drained seafood, bell pepper, onion, coriander, reserved rind, and mayonnaise. Toss the mixture gently to coat it lightly with the mayonnaise. Arrange the salad on a platter lined with the lettuce leaves and garnish it with the reserved orange slices and the additional coriander. Serves 4 as a luncheon entree, or 6 as a first course.

Short Bread Sandwich Cookies

7 ounces unsalted butter
Pinch of salt
1 teaspoon vanilla
⅓ cup sugar
3 egg yolks
2 cups all-purpose flour, sifted
6 ounces chocolate
2 tablespoons butter
1 ½ heavy cream

Preheat oven to 350 ° F.

Cream butter, add salt, vanilla and sugar and beat until fluffy. Add yolks and beat until smooth. Add flour on low speed and beat only to incorporate. Pat into 2 round disks and refrigerate, wrapped in plastic wrap until firm. Cut into rounds and bake for approximately 12 to 15 minutes. Do not allow to burn.

Filling:
Melt chocolate with butter. Remove from heat and wisk in heavy cream. Let stand until mixture cools and begins to thicken. Use a generous tablespoon of filling for each cookie. Sandwich together with filling and allow to set. May be dusted with confectioners sugar.

AUSTRALIAN OPEN

Plantation Catering
Newport, Rhode Island

PASTA SALAD WITH NOISETTES OF LAMB

COPPER CARROTS

TREACLE CAKE WITH APPLE SAUCE

Pasta Salad with Noisettes of Lamb

Warm bowtie pasta tossed with olive oil and parmesan cheese on a bed of cold Italian parsley, topped with lamb, nicoise olives,and a dash of sherry wine vinegar. The lamb can be prepared ahead and served at room temperature, or warm if you prefer.

Sherry Vinaigrette:
½ cup sherry wine vinegar
⅓ cup light olive oil
⅓ cup walnut oil
1 teaspoon chopped shallots

Combine all ingredients. Enough for 4 salads.

Copper Carrots

1 pound baby carrots, peeled and trimmed
2 tablespoons unsalted butter
2 tablespoons orange juice
2 tablespoons honey
½ teaspoon curry powder
Salt and pepper to taste

Cook carrots in boiling water until barely tender. Drain vegetables well and place in a shallow baking dish. Melt butter in saucepan and stir in orange juice, honey and curry. Heat to boiling and cook 1 minute. Pour over carrots. Bake in 400 degree oven until carrots are slightly glazed, about 15 minutes. Serves 4- 5.

Treacle Cake with Cinnamon Applesauce

2¾ cups all-purpose flour
1 tablespoon ground ginger

2 teaspoons cinnamon
½ teaspoon freshly grated nutmeg
1 teaspoon ground allspice
½ teaspoon salt
1 cup vegetable shortening at room temperature
1½ cups firmly packed dark brown sugar
1 cup dark unsulfured molasses
2 teaspoons baking soda
4 large eggs
Powdered sugar for sifting over cake
Cinnamon applesauce (recipe follows) as an accompaniment

In a bowl sift together the flour, ginger, cinnamon, nutmeg, allspice, and salt. In separate bowl cream shortening with an electric mixer , add the brown sugar and beat the mixture until it is light and fluffy. Add the molasses in a stream and beat the mixture until it is combined well. In a measuring cup stir the baking soda into ⅔ cup boiling water. Add this mixture to the molasses mixture in a stream, beating. (The batter will separate at this point.) Add the flour mixture and the eggs and beat until it is just combined. Pour batter into a buttered and floured 10-inch springform pan and bake the cake in the lower third of a pre-heated 350° F oven for 1 hour and 5 minutes to 1 hour and 10 minutes, or until the tester comes out clean. Let cake cool in the pan for 5 minutes, remove from pan and let cool completely. (The cake improves in flavor if made 24 hours in advance.) Invert the cake on a serving plate. Put a paper doily on top of it, and sift the powdered sugar over the doily. Remove the doily carefully and serve the cake with the cinnamon applesauce.

Cinnamon Applesauce

2 tablespoons unsalted butter
4 McIntosh Apples, sliced but not peeled or cored
2 to 3 tablespoons sugar -- to taste
¼ teaspoon cinnamon

In a heavy skillet, melt the butter over moderate heat. Add the apples and stir them to coat them with butter. Stir in water, sugar, and cinnamon. Simmer the mixture, covered, for 20 minutes, stirring occasionally. Puree the mixture through a food mill fitted with a coarse blade, into a bowl and serve it warm with cake. Makes 2 cups.

FRENCH OPEN

Plantation Catering
Newport, Rhode Island

ASPARAGUS WITH GINGER VINAIGRETTE

SHRIMP WITH CORNMEAL SAVARINS

STRAWBERRY NAPOLEON

Asparagus with Ginger Vinaigrette

20-25 Asparagus (5-6 per serving)
1 cup salad oil
¼ cup lemon juice
½ cup champagne vinegar
1 tablespoon grated ginger
1 tablespoon dijon mustard
Salt and pepper to taste

Steam asparagus and rinse under cold water to stop cooking. Combine all ingredients except salad oil, then whisk in oil while pouring in a steady stream. Pour over asparagus at last moment. Serves 5-6.

Shrimp with Cornmeal Savarins

½ cup cornmeal
1½ teaspoons baking powder
¼ teaspoon baking soda
2 teaspoons sugar
¼ teaspoon salt
¼ cup all-purpose flour
1 egg yolk, beaten
2 tablespoons butter, melted
¼ cup heavy cream
½ cup buttermilk
1 egg white
¼ cup corn kernels
2 tablespoons red or green peppers, minced
1 tablespoon jalapeno peppers, minced
2 tablespoons Monterey Jack cheese, grated

Sift together the cornmeal, baking powder, baking soda, salt and flour. Combine the egg yolk, butter, cream and buttermilk, and stir into cornmeal mixture just until incorporated. Beat the egg white until soft peaks form and fold into cornmeal mixture. Fold in the peppers, corn and cheese.
Divide among 6 well-greased savarin molds at 400 ° F for 15 minutes or until a toothpick will come out clean.

Strawberry Napoleon

1½ pounds puff pastry

Pastry Cream:
3 yolks
½ cup sugar
2 tablespoons flour
1 cup milk
1 teaspoon vanilla
butter, as needed
¾ cup heavy cream
1 tablespoon powdered sugar
1 pound fresh strawberries
Sugar, as needed

Scald milk. Beat yolks and sugar together until light in color and thick. Beat in flour, gradually add hot milk, stir over low heat constantly until thick. Boil 1 minute. Strain into bowl and fold in vanilla. Rub surface with butter to keep skin from forming as it cools.

Roll out dough into three 8" x 12" rectangles about 1/16" thick. Square off edges with knife. Place on baking sheet that has been greased and spritzed with water. Cover and chill for one hour. Prick all over with fork. Bake 20 minutes at 425° F. Cool on sheets.

Beat cream with powdered sugar until soft peaks form. Set aside. Reserve 6 or 8 perfect berries for garnish. Slice remaining strawberries and sprinkle lightly with sugar.

To assemble: Spread pastry cream on one rectangle of pastry. Cover with second layer of pastry, cover this layer with ½ of the whipped cream and spread the fruit on top. Place the last layer of pastry on top and decorate with whipped cream and whole strawberries.

WIMBLEDON

*Plantation Catering,
Newport, Rhode Island*

STILTON AND WALNUT TART

COD FISH CAKES WITH
CHIVE MAYONNAISE

ENGLISH TRIFLE WITH
SUMMER BERRIES AND CREAM

Stilton and Walnut Tarts

2 recipes cream cheese pastry dough (recipe follows)
⅔ cup walnuts, ground, plus 14 lightly toasted walnut halves for
**   garnish**
Raw rice for weighting the shells
1¼ cups half and half
6 ounces Stilton, crumbled
3 large eggs
Watercress sprigs for garnish

Roll half the dough into ⅛" thick rectangle on a floured surface, fit it into a 14" by 4½" inch rectangular flan form, set on a baking sheet, and fold the edges inward, crimping them decoratively. Prepare another shell with remaining dough in the same manner. (Alternatively, the shells may be made in two 9 inch tart pans with removable fluted rims.) Sprinkle the ground walnuts evenly in the pie shells and press them gently into the dough. Prick the bottom of the shells lightly with a fork and chill the shells for 30 minutes. Line the shells with foil, fill the foil with rice, and bake the shells in the lower third of a preheated oven at 425 ° F for 10 minutes. Remove the rice and foil carefully, bake the shells for 5 to 6 minutes more, or until they are golden, and let them cool on the baking sheets on racks.

In a saucepan combine the half and half and the Stilton, bring the liquid to a simmer and stir the mixture until the Stilton is just melted. Remove the pan from the heat and let the mixture cool. In a bowl whisk together the Stilton mixture and the eggs, divide the mixture into the shells, and bake tarts in the middle of a preheated 375 ° F oven for 30 to 35 minutes, or until a knife inserted in the custard ½ inch from the edge comes out clean. (The custard may not be fully set in the center but will continue to cook after the tarts are removed from the oven.) Let the tarts cool to room temperature and remove the flan forms carefully. Transfer the tarts to platters, garnish them with the walnut halves, and garnish the platters with the watercress. To serve the tarts, halve them lengthwise and cut them crosswise into sevenths. Makes 28 hors d' oeuvres.

Cream Cheese Pastry Dough:
¾ stick (6 tablespoons) cold unsalted butter, cut into bits
4 ounces cold cream cheese
1 cup all-purpose flour
½ teaspoon salt

In a food processor blend the butter, the cream cheese, the flour, and the salt, pulsing the motor, until the dough just begins to form a ball, gather the dough into a ball and flatten it slightly. Dust the dough with flour and chill it, wrapped in plastic wrap, for 1 hour. Dough may be made in advance and kept wrapped well and chilled.

COD FISH CAKES WITH CHIVE MAYONNAISE

½ pound boiling potatoes
½ stick (¼ cup) unsalted butter
Freshly grated nutmeg to taste
2 onions, chopped fine
2 cloves garlic, minced
1 carrot, chopped
½ cup dry white wine
1 pound cod fillet
⅔ cup minced fresh parsley leaves
1 heaping tablespoon snipped fresh dill or 1 teaspoon dried
3 large whole eggs
1 large egg yolk
All-purpose flour for dredging
2 cups fine dry bread crumbs
1 cup vegetable oil

In a small saucepan combine the potatoes with enough cold water to cover them by 1 inch, bring the water to a boil, and simmer the potatoes, covered for 15 minutes, or until they are tender. Drain the potatoes, return them to the pan, and steam them, covered, over moderate heat, shaking the pan, for 30 seconds to evaporate any excess water. Peel the potatoes, force them through a ricer or a food mill fitted with the medium disk into a bowl. Stir in one tablespoon of the butter, the nutmeg, and salt and pepper to taste. In a heavy saucepan saute half the onions, the carrot, and the celery in one tablespoon of the remaining butter over moderately high heat, stirring for 5 minutes. Add 4 cups of water and the wine, bring the liquid to a boil, and simmer the mixture for 20 minutes. Add the cod and poach it just until it flakes. Transfer the cod with a slotted spoon to a cutting board, discard any skin and let it cool. In a small heavy skillet cook the remaining onions in the remaining 2 tablespoons butter over moderately low heat, stirring occasionally, until they are softened. Let them cool. To the potato mixture add the flaked cod, the onion mixture, the parsley, the dill, 1 of the whole eggs, the yolk, and salt and pepper to taste. Combine the mixture well and chill it, covered, for one hour.

In three shallow bowls, place the flour, the remaining 2 whole eggs, beaten lightly, and the bread crumbs. Form rounded tablespoons of the cod mixture into balls the size of golf balls (the mixture will flatten into cakes as it is coated). Dredge each in flour, dip in egg and coat with crumbs. Transfer the cod cakes to a jelly-roll pan lined with wax paper and chill them, uncovered, for at least 30 minutes and up to 6 hours.

In a heavy skillet large enough to hold the cod cakes without crowding them, heat the oil over moderately high heat. Fry cakes until undersides are crisp and golden, turn and repeat. Transfer the cod cakes with a slotted spatula to paper towels to drain and serve the chive mayonnaise.

Chive Mayonnaise:
4 scallions, chopped fine, greens included
1 shallot, minced
Freshly ground pepper to taste
¾ cup mayonnaise
½ cup sour cream
2 tablespoons Dijon mustard

Combine all ingredients.

English Trifle

Genoise Ingredients:
6 eggs, room temperature
⅔ cup sugar
1 cup flour, sifted
1 teaspoon vanilla
3 tablespoons butter, melted (cooled)

Filling:
4 cups berries
Strawberry jam
Sherry

Beat eggs with sugar until the mixture falls from the beater in a ribbon. Fold in flour, then butter and vanilla, being careful not to deflate the batter. Bake in 2 8-inch cake pans, buttered, floured and lined with parchment paper at 350 ° F for 25 minutes or until golden brown on top and cake begins to pull away from sides of pan. Remove from oven, cool 10 minutes in pan, then remove to wire rack to cool completely.

Custard Sauce:
3 cups milk
3 cups heavy cream
12 egg yolks
1 cup sugar
1 tablespoon vanilla

Scald milk and heavy cream together. Beat yolks with sugar until pale and thick. Slowly add scalded milk mixture. Cook over low heat stirring constantly, until mixture is thickened and coats the back of a spoon. Overcooking will cause the sauce to curdle. Remove from heat. Add vanilla and cool.

To assemble trifle:
Split one 8-inch layer of cake in half, place in bottom of trifle bowl, trimming to fit if necessary. Brush with sherry, then spread with thin layer of jam. Sprinkle an even layer of berries across top. Pour 1 cup of custard sauce on top. Repeat process with remaining cake and berries. Refrigerate overnight. Cover with plastic wrap. To serve garnish with berries and whipped cream and extra custard sauce if desired.

US OPEN

Plantation Catering
Newport, Rhode Island

CHEDDAR STRAWS

LOBSTER AND MELON SALAD
(SERVED IN A MELON HALF)

IRISH LEMON PUDDING

GINGER ICE TEA

Cheddar Straws

1½ pound puff pastry chilled
1 beaten egg
1 cup cheddar or other hard cheese, grated

Roll the puff pastry into a rectangle approximately 30 inches by 8 inches thick. Using a sharp knife and yardstick, trim to precise shape. Cut lengthwise into 2 pieces. Brush with beaten egg and sprinkle liberally with cheese. Cut into 1 inch strips. Lift with spatula and place on a baking sheet. Refrigerate, covered with wax paper and allow to rest 45 minutes. Preheat oven to 400 degrees. Bake 10 minutes then reduce heat to 350 degrees and bake 15-20 minutes longer or until light brown. Place on rack to cool. Yield 60 pieces.

Lobster and Melon Salad

1 pound lobster meat cut into chunks
    (save claws to decorate)
4 cups melon balls --
    honeydew, cranshaw, Persian cantaloupe, etc.

Dressing:
1 cup mayonnaise, preferably homemade
1 tablespoon vermouth
1 tablespoon poupon mustard
1 teaspoon balsamic vinegar
1 tablespoon minced fresh basil
2 tablespoons minced scallions

Combine ingredients: in each melon half, place approximately 2 tablespoons of dressing, fill with melon balls and arrange lobster meat over top of melon.

Left: Entrance doors at the
International Tennis Hall of Fame
Photo by Ron Manville

Irish Lemon Pudding

½ cup softened butter
1½ cups sugar
6 eggs, separated
⅔ cup lemon juice
⅔ cup all purpose flour
2 tablespoons grated lemon zest
½ teaspoon salt
3 cups milk
Pinch cream of tartar

Preheat oven to 325° F. Grease a 12 cup souffle dish.

Cream the butter and sugar together. Beat in 6 egg yolks, one at a time until incorporated. Mixture should be light and fluffy. On low speed add lemon juice. Stir in flour, lemon zest and salt. Whisk in milk, beating slowly.

In a separate bowl beat the egg whites with cream of tartar until stiff but not dry. Fold into lemon mixture. Pour into souffle dish and bake for 50-55 minutes until pudding is fluffy and golden brown on top. Serve sprinkled with sifted confectioners sugar.

Ginger Tea

8 tea bags of almond herbal tea
16 slices crystallized ginger

Boil enough fresh water for 8 cups of tea. Place tea bags and 8 slices of ginger into teapot and add boiling water. Steep for 6 to 8 minutes. Remove tea bags and ginger. Refrigerate until well chilled. Fill a tall glass with shaved ice. Pour gingered tea into glass and garnish with a slice of ginger. This tea is an excellent digestive.

TRAINING
TIPS

*W*e all need to stay fit, and what better way to obtain the benefits of exercise than by playing a vigorous game of tennis. Matched with proper eating habits, regular games of tennis can produce better health and help prevent heart and vascular diseases. And, just as important, regular exercise helps us feel more alert and more appreciative of the good things life brings us.

Before you start any exercise program, consider your physical capabilities, goals and schedule. Choose exercises that you'll enjoy doing and that will build up your strength and endurance. Don't limit yourself to one form of exercise; no single one develops total fitness. Several are necessary for well-rounded development.

With that in mind we have collected some training tips from a few athletes and coaches. We thought you might like to use some of these in your fitness program.

Preceding page: Surbiton Lawn Tennis Tournament trophy
Surrey Championship Ladies Singles
Photo by John Hopf

Michael S. Estep

Tennis Pro, former coach of Martina Navratilova

Every player should take time out from tennis to play other sports. Tennis is a very frustrating sport -- for the amateur as well as the professional. The professional must take time off to replenish the mind and, at the same time, rebuild the body. Cross training (or playing/exercising) in other sports is necessary. For the amateur, an appreciation for tennis can be best cultivated by occasionally playing other sports for recreation. Playing other sports will frequently help his or her tennis game, as well.

Generally speaking, a tennis player's hand and arm cannot be too strong. Many poor strokes are a result of a weak wrist, grip or forearm. There are many methods that are useful for building up one's arm, but the safest and surest method is simply swinging a racquet as fast as one can, back and forth, simulating a typical forehand or backhand volley without a ball. Typically, one should "last" between 1 and 3 minutes before reaching "failure." Failure can be described as the feeling of "I just can't go anymore!" After waiting a few minutes, the player should try the exercise one more time (usually lasting half the time as the first simulated volley). This exercise done 2 to 4 times a day can have a great effect on one's game in one week's time.

René Lacoste

Tennis Hall of Famer

What are my favorite dishes? You will probably be surprised by my answer! I shall not give you the recipe of some of the elaborate dishes - with cream, butter and other ingredients that many foreigners like to taste when visiting France.

My favorite dishes today are simply grilled lobster and "macaroni au gratin" with a brown crust of gruyere cheese on top.

But at a time when there is much talk of the Lendl eating regime, it may interest you to know what I was eating in 1927, for instance, when I played the U.S. championship in Forest Hills.

I started the day with a huge breakfast, which included an omelet, tomatoes, Virginia ham, corn flakes and plenty of buttered toast with marmalade. I felt that all of these calories were needed for me to regenerate from five matches played in hot weather without rest between games and points (as allowed today) and without tie breaks. Besides we had no air conditioners and perspired a lot during nights spent in the Old Vanderbilt Hotel!

For luncheon I loved seafood: clams and blue fish, or lobster salad. I remember having lunch with Billy Johnston just before motoring to Forest Hills to meet him in the afternoon. He said he expected to beat me after seeing me eat lobster salad and milk, which he felt was a dangerous combination.

For dinner I loved small spring chicken or beef and my favorite American dish -- apple tart with cream.

I forgot to mention, in the morning and sometimes before going to sleep, I would drink a lot of orange juice, as advised by my mother, because of the high amount of vitamin C (instead of today's pills).

Later traveling in the states, I had the pleasure to stay with Mr. and Mrs. Kingman, then president of the USLTA. I remember Mrs. Kingman's Thanksgiving roast turkey as a marvelous dish.

Reading over what I have written, I note that I omitted to mention that I had cream with my corn flakes. Today, in order to keep my 1927 weight unchanged, I still eat corn flakes but with low fat milk. I hope this will help you or at least amuse you.

Ivan Lendl

Number one tennis player in 4 of the past 6 years

I always have a meal of pasta and sauce with chicken, veal or seafood the night before an important match. I will also have soup to start and a lot of whole grain bread. The day of the match, if time permits, I will eat a bowl of pasta. If time is short, I will have a quite a few chicken sandwiches.

The whole idea is to load up on carbohydrates so that if a match is long and strenuous, my body will have enough carbohydrates stored to convert them into the energy I need.

Doug McKenney

Strength and conditioning coach for the Hartford Whalers

Nutrition is one component most programs of sports conditioning overlook. The following sections will provide information on how to obtain sufficient nutrients and energy for intense physical activity and lose weight, if necessary. Excess weight in the form of fat reduces speed and endurance. Nutrition is one of the key factors in lowering fat and stabilizing or increasing muscle tissue.

During training, the body must recuperate between workouts to reach higher levels of fitness. Often, lack of progress or "staleness" during training can be related to poor nutritional lifestyle and not the training program.

A balanced diet is achieved by modifying current eating habits. The diet should approximate 60% complex carbohydrates, 20-25% fat, and 12-15% protein. The following are guidelines to achieve this combination.

A. *Have daily servings from the four major Food Groups:*
    Recommended servings per day: Grain Products, 4; Fruits   and vegetables, 4; Dairy products, 3; Meat, fish and poultry, 2.
This approach will help you achieve variety in your diet. It is interesting to note a total of 8 servings should come from grain products, fruits and vegetables. This allows for a high percentage of the total caloric intake to be from carbohydrates.

B. *Eat 3 meals per day.* When weight gain is desired, there should be an addition of 2 to 3 snacks. It is important to keep food intake at a constant level throughout the day to maintain muscle tissue, promote reduction of body fat and reduce sluggishness and fatigue. In addition, an evenly distributed caloric intake through the day keeps the body's ability to burn calories elevated. Skipping meals to lose weight is counterproductive and will not allow for progress in the training program.

C. *Cut down on the foods that are high in fat:*
    1. Red meats (steak, hamburger, franks, luncheon meats, etc.)
    2. Pork products (bacon and sausage)
    3. Whole milk, ice cream , cream and cream sauces
    4. Cheese and cheese sauces
    5. Butter or margarine
    6. Mayonnaise or miracle whip
    7. Oils of all kinds (used in cooking or salads)
    8. Salad dressings
    9. French fries or other forms of fried potatoes such as chips
A diet that is high in fat and low in carbohydrates slows the process of energy storage in the muscle, leading to less fuel for high intensity activity.

D. *Change eating habits to lower fat intake:*
    1. Buy lean cuts of red meat (flank steak or London broil) and trim all excess fat.
    2. Keep meats to moderate servings. When possible, substitute fish and poultry for meat.
    3. Don't fry foods: bake, broil, boil, poach, steam, barbecue, or microwave.

4. Use all fats sparingly (oil, butter, margarine, mayonnaise and miracle whip).

5. Use sparingly all dairy products made with whole milk.

6. Avoid products packed in oil.

7. Substitute foods that will help to lower your fat intake:

    A. Low-cal salad dressing, no oil salad dressing

    B. Low-cal mayonnaise

    C. Low-cal margarine

    D. Skim or low-fat milk products

    E. Tuna packed in water

8. Buy low-fat products in general.

E. *Increase intake of complex carbohydrates and grain products.* Foods such as breads, rolls, cereals, pancakes, waffles, french toast, pasta, rice, vegetables, fruit and fruit juices are high in vitamins and minerals and have high water content, jellies and jams.

F. *Refined sugars should not replace balanced meals (sweets, soda, candies, cakes, etc).* Sweets high in fat are not good sources of carbohydrates for replenishing muscle energy stores. Moreover, foods that are high in refined sugar have lower vitamin and mineral content, and many sweets are also high in fat.

G. *Water intake should be 4-6 glasses a day.* This amount of water is necessary to avoid the effects of dehydration: fatigue, deterioration in performance, and increase in body temperature and muscle pulls. Thirst is usually a reliable guide to the need for water. But, because of tension, anxiety and large sweat losses, thirst is an inaccurate indicator of water need during competition. Athletes should be encouraged to weigh themselves before and after training to determine the amount of fluid that needs to be replaced. A 3% weight loss leads to impaired performance; a 5% loss can result in some signs of heat exhaustion; a 7% loss may produce hallucinations and put the individual in the danger zone. Fluid intake before and during the event will not fully replace fluid losses, but partial replacement reduces the risk of overheating. After the event, the athlete should continue to drink at frequent intervals until the weight has been regained.

H. *Drink alcohol moderately.* Alcohol can impair your reaction time, hand-eye coordination, accuracy and balance. It also can impair body temperature regulation and cause dehydration. Moreover, it decreases strength, power, local muscular endurance, speed and cardiovascular endurance and hinders muscle growth. Only 7% of the daily caloric intake should come from alcoholic beverages.

Are large amounts of protein essential to an athlete during vigorous training? For athletes who want to gain muscle mass there is no evidence that protein supplementation of the diet is necessary. When the diet is balanced, there is enough energy for intense training and protein for growth and repair. The National Research Council on Nutrition has stated that 1gm/day of protein per 2.2

Right: Center Court Match Play
International Tennis Hall of Fame
Photo by Ron Manville

lbs. of body weight is sufficient for both athletes and non-athletes. High levels of dietary protein may increase the tendency to accumulate body fat. Also, excess dietary protein produces increased urinary water loss as excess waste products are removed.

Are vitamin and mineral supplements necessary?
Increased food consumption ensures adequate intake of those vitamins and minerals that are depleted during strenuous exercise. If the food intake is not adequate, energy storage in the muscle will not be 100%. Regardless of excess vitamins, there first must be fuel to start the process of energy release for exercise.

Usually there is no need for mineral supplements. An adequate supply of minerals is present in a well-balanced diet, but if the diet is not balanced, then mineral supplementation might prove beneficial. Heavy exercise causes sweating, which can deplete the body's store of sodium, potassium and other minerals. Potassium deficiency can result in muscle cramping. This can be avoided by including potassium-rich foods in the diet, such as bananas and oranges.

Ingestion of salt tablets to replace sodium losses is seldom necessary and may be dangerous. Only in prolonged activity associated with intense sweating lasting more than a week is additional salt needed. Any supplementation of the diet should be preceded by a computer analysis so the need for the nutrients in question can be evaluated.

Stan Smith

Tennis Hall of Famer

One of the most important things in preparing for a tournament or individual match in very hot weather is to make sure you are properly hydrated. You should drink plenty of water the night before and the morning of the match. This will help prevent cramping, as well as loss of energy and even concentration. As for eating, everyone is different, but I suggest eating at least two hours before the match. Choose foods that will be easy to digest. This means staying away from red meat or greasy food and eating carbohydrates including fruits. Perhaps most important is a consistency in eating so that you don't eat anything before a big match that you do not normally eat.

Bill Toomey

1968 U. S. Olympic Gold Medal winner in the Decathalon

An athlete must always be in control of his or her competitive and training environment to be successful. To plan for your competitive moment, you must understand your nutritional needs in terms of energy, food (especially complex carbohydrates) and fluid replacements. Avoid foods that are difficult to digest before, during and directly after a serious energy drain. Many athletes forsake their good habits after the competition and, thereby, delay valuable repair and rest for the body.

Training before one's biggest competition should be dramatically reduced so that the entire body can overcome any remnants of fatigue. Too many athletes "leave it on the training field" before the competition.

A valuable tool that I employed in the late '60s was visualization of the time, pace and competition awaiting me. I marked off the dates on the calendar and began visualizing myself as physically and mentally perfect on the competition days. In spite of knee surgeries, pulled muscles, hepatitis and mononucleosis, I never missed a national championship and won five in a row.

Mentally, an athlete must be totally selfish during the moment of competition. He or she must be willing to avoid all negative cues and practice concentrating on the task at hand. One must become a competitive animal. Forget your problems and go for it!

Lastly, the injury crutch is one to avoid. Do not talk about your injuries with anyone. Do not abuse training with the need for massages before competitions, as they will drain you.

The day of competition, do not think about your event emotionally until the moment occurs. Save the adrenalin -- it's powerful, but limited.

INDEX BY CELEBRITY

INDEX

CONVERSION CHART

U.S. and Metric Measurements and Equivalents

60 drops = 1 teaspoon = ⅙ ounce = 5 milliliters
1 teaspoon = ⅓ tablespoon = ⅙ ounce = 5 milliliters
1½ teaspoons = ½ tablespoon = ¼ ounce = 7.5 milliliters
3 teaspoons = 1 tablespoon = ½ ounce = 15 milliliters
1 tablespoon = 3 teaspoons = ½ ounce = 15 milliliters
2 tablespoons = ⅛ cup = 1 ounce = 30 milliliters = 30 grams
4 tablespoons = ¼ cup = 2 ounces = 60 milliliters = 60 grams
5⅓ tablespoons = ⅓ cup = 2.6 ounces = 80 milliliters
8 tablespoons = ½ cup = 4 ounces = 120 milliliters = 115 grams
10⅔ tablespoons = ⅔ cup = 5.3 ounces = 160 milliliters
12 tablespoons = ¾ cup = 6 ounces = 180 milliliters = 180 grams
16 tablespoons = 1 cup = 8 ounces = 240 milliliters = 225 grams
⅓ cup = 5 tablespoons plus 1 teaspoon = 1.3 ounces = 55 milliliters
¼ cup = 4 tablespoons = 2 ounces = 60 milliliters = 60 grams
⅜ cup = 6 tablespoons = 3 ounces = 90 milliliters
½ cup = 8 tablespoons = 4 ounces = 120 milliliters = 115 grams
⅝ cup = 10 tablespoons = 5 ounces = 150 milliliters
⅔ cup = 10 tablespoons plus 2 teaspoons = 5.3 ounces = 177 milliliters
¾ cup = 12 tablespoons = 6 ounces = 180 milliliters = 180 grams
⅞ cup = ¾ cup plus 2 tablespoons = 7 ounces = 210 milliliters
1 cup = 16 tablespoons = 8 ounces = ½ pint = 240 milliliters = 225 grams
2 cups = 16 ounces = 1 pint = 480 milliliters or .473 liters = 450 grams
1 quart = 4 cups = 32 ounces = 2 pints = 960 milliliters or .95 liter = 900 grams
1.06 quarts = 33.8 ounces = 1 liter
1 gallon = 16 cups = 128 ounces = 4 quarts = 3.8 liters

Temperature conversions °Fahrenheit (F) to °Celsius (C)

-10°F = -23 °C (freezer storage)
0°F = -17.7 °C
32°F = 0 °C (water freezes)
50°F = 10 °C
68°F = 20 °C (room temperature)
205°F = 96.1 °C (water simmers)
212°F = 100 °C (water boils)
350°F = 177 °C (baking)
400°F = 204.4 °C (hot oven)
450°F = 232 °C (very hot oven)
500°F = 260 °C (broiling)

CELEBRITIES SERVE

CHEFS TO THE COURT
28 Mt. Vernon Street
Newport, R.I.   02840

Please send me _____ copies of CELEBRITIES SERVE at $15.95 per copy plus $4.00 for shipping and handling. Rhode Island residents please add $1.12 per copy for sales tax.

Enclosed is my check in the amount of $ _____

Name _____

Address _____

City _____ State _____ Zip _____

FROM: CHEFS TO THE COURT
28 Mt. Vernon Street
Newport, R.I. 02840

TO:

Name _____

Address _____

City _____ State ____ Zip ____

MAILING LABEL - PLEASE PRINT

CELEBRITIES SERVE

CHEFS TO THE COURT
28 Mt. Vernon Street
Newport, R.I.   02840

Please send me _____ copies of CELEBRITIES SERVE at $15.95 per copy plus $4.00 for shipping and handling. Rhode Island residents please add $1.12 per copy for sales tax.

Enclosed is my check in the amount of $ _____

Name _____

Address _____

City _____ State _____ Zip _____

FROM: CHEFS TO THE COURT
28 Mt. Vernon Street
Newport, R.I. 02840

TO:

Name _____

Address _____

City _____ State ____ Zip ____

MAILING LABEL - PLEASE PRINT

CELEBRITIES SERVE

CHEFS TO THE COURT
28 Mt. Vernon Street
Newport, R.I.   02840

Please send me _____ copies of CELEBRITIES SERVE at $15.95 per copy plus $4.00 for shipping and handling. Rhode Island residents please add $1.12 per copy for sales tax.

Enclosed is my check in the amount of $ _____

Name _____

Address _____

City _____ State _____ Zip _____

MAKE CHECKS PAYABLE TO: CHEFS TO THE COURT

FROM: CHEFS TO THE COURT
28 Mt. Vernon Street
Newport, R.I. 02840

TO:

Name _____

Address _____

City _____ State ____ Zip ____

MAILING LABEL - PLEASE PRINT